THE HIDDEN PASSPORT

My Childhood Journey Through
Japanese Concentration Camps in Java

Phyllis Pilgrim

For: Leslie
with blessings on your
Inner Journey
with love
Phyllis Pilgrim

THE HIDDEN PASSPORT
My Childhood Journey Through Japanese Concentration Camps in Java
Phyllis Pilgrim

First published in the United States of America, September 2009

ISBN 978-0-578-03056-2
Library of Congress Control Number 2009907252

Printed in the United States of America

FRONT COVER IMAGE
Phyllis Pilgrim at age two, held by a passenger on the P. & O. Liner from
the Netherlands to the Dutch East Indies. Phyllis' family did not imagine at that
time that they would end up in Japanese concentration camps for several years.

BACK COVER IMAGES
Handkerchiefs embroidered by Phyllis' mother Dorothy Nisbet with the names
of the women and children in the first prison camp in Java, 1942.

BOOK & COVER DESIGN
Michelle Haymoz, Encinitas, California, www.michellehaymoz.com

CHAPTER ILLUSTRATION
Rosemary KimBal, Cardiff by the Sea, California, www.dancingbrush.com

CONTACT & BOOK ORDERS
www.thehiddenpassport.com
www.phyllispilgrim.com
Ordering by phone 1-800-247-6553

With gratitude

to my mother Dorothy Nisbet for her outspokenness and honesty,

and to my father Frank Nisbet for the gentle man that he was

and for his steadfastness.

Without their stories I would not have mine.

ACKNOWLEDGMENTS

It has taken me twenty-five years to gradually unearth the deeply in-grained memories and effects of my childhood years lived as "guests of the Japanese" during World War II in Japanese concentration camps in Java. This book is the result of many taped conversations with my mother and friends, and subsequent edits of the stories to get to those memories as remembered by a child aged five to nine years old, alongside those of my mother's adult memories almost fifty years after the events.

I have my mother to thank for her willingness to retell her mem-ories of those difficult times. I have more than five hours of taped conversations with her, some including my father's memories before he died in 1991. My mother is still alive at age ninety-seven living in a retirement home in Dumfries to be near her son, my brother, Donald. I thank her for her honesty and courage.

I thank my father for agreeing to finally tell his experience on tape, albeit superficially, without any expression of deep anguish which he must have felt during those impossible years separated from his family. I regret I did not have the opportunity or the wit to ask him about his feelings during that time. I can only imagine.

Also many thanks to my brother, Donald Nisbet, who experienced the war as a little boy aged two to six years old and, after reading my book, nudged a few more memories out of me as well as shared the few he could remember. I thank him for the care he gives my mother now by visiting her in the retirement home near to where he lives in Dumfries.

My gratitude to Deborah Szekely, founder of Rancho la Puerta, for creating an exquisite place for me and many others to work and grow professionally and personally over the past twenty-seven years. The Ranch gave me the space and place to meet many wonderful people and to write my story. Thank you.

I give thanks to Debbie Burger for transcribing hours of tape into the computer. Her help saved me hours of time and gave me an invaluable jumpstart to write the book.

I give thanks to my writer friends at Rancho La Puerta over the past twenty years who gave me encouragement to "tell my story," who read my original transcripts and gave me advice on how to martial the material. Teaching me to "show, not tell" to add color and depth to my story, with tips on how to "make a statement" to catch the reader's interest, was the best advice from Rita Jacobs, Marilyn Mason, Joyce Chapman, Dan Wakefield, April Smith, and Irene Borger. Their writing workshops conducted at the Ranch inspired me to dig deeper and write from my heart as well as my mind.

Friends who read my various drafts gave me invaluable insights to flesh out the story by asking pertinent questions about the historical setting of that time and what emotions I felt in certain situations: Paul and Evelyn Dodd, Molly Crowcroft, Michele Hebert, Olive Hebert, Jennifer Fox, Paul Gould, and Antonia Allegra.

My gratitude to my copy editor, Iris Bass. Those final touches are so important for the accuracy of the book.

My appreciation to graphic designer Michelle Haymoz for her creativity and knowledge in designing the layout and cover of the book, and getting it into print. It was a wonderful journey working with her.

My thanks to Rosemary KimBal for her exquisite Calligraphy, and to Pat Harrison for her lovely portrait photography of me.

I give heartfelt thanks to my editor Arlene Matthews, who helped me shape my final story over the past year, and who encouraged me to keep rereading it and to come up with more camp memories interconnected to my adult life's choices. There is so much unremembered I am sure. Her encouragement kept me going. She is a gem. Thank you, Arlene.

And finally, I give all those I have not mentioned by name my thanks for their encouragement, interest and ideas. I have been inspired by many people over the past twenty-five years to write this book.

CONTENTS

Introduction

Barbados 1979

From the age of five to nine years old I, along with my mother and younger brother, was a World War II prisoner in four different Japanese concentration camps on the island of Java. The ingrained experiences at so young an age were never discussed in my family during my teenage or young adult years growing up in postwar Britain. Whatever fears and frustrations I harbored during those war years were at a deeply subconscious level that undoubtedly affected my choices and behaviors in my adult life. It all came to a head thirty-four years after the war's end. The difficulties of life in Barbados, where I was living and working with my husband, Torrey, in 1979, brought these hidden suppressed conditionings to the surface.

At the end of a long day of working as a geography teacher in a government grammar school, I came home to the Yoga Center, where my husband ordered me to sweep the yoga and dining rooms immediately—yet another task added to my already full schedule of work at the business we managed together. This was not the first time he had ordered me about; it had happened hundreds, perhaps thousands of times. I had never questioned his authority, or anyone's authority. But today it hit me forcibly: I don't know whether it was my husband's manner of speech, his overbearing tone, his demands on my time and energy, the lack of a warm greeting (no "How was

1

your day?"), or the absence of respect for my welfare and well-being, but it was the straw that broke the camel's back. Something snapped. I heard myself say, "This marriage is worse than any Japanese concentration camp." I was stunned at my own statement.

I realized in a flash of understanding that this was the real crossroads in my adult life, after twenty-three years of marriage. It was the watershed between living unconsciously with little understanding for consequences, just living life the best way I knew how, and living with more awareness—making conscious choices for a more satisfying and happy existence. My whole life ran before my eyes, and I suddenly knew where I was and what I was doing. It was then that I had the first realization that deep-seated memories of the concentration camps were affecting my adulthood, with many unhappy consequences.

I now asked myself, "Why?" Over the previous ten years, I had done more and more at the Yoga Center, until I was relentlessly occupied from 6 a.m. to midnight, seven days of the week. My husband frequently told newcomers to the center, "My wife does not pull her weight around here." Any protest on my part resulted in a rage on his. I had learned to keep quiet and just do what was required. But I knew that this moment augured the end of my married relationship.

Until that revelation, I constantly ameliorated situations of stress and arguments, in the interests of our health and sanity. I considered marriage sacred, not to be given up lightly. If only I could find the magic key to make us both happy. It was my job to change me, since I knew I could not change him.

The demands of running the business of the Yoga Center were end-less and constant. The jobs ranged from running a vegetarian restau-rant to transplanting seedlings in the organic garden, from training local women to cook healthful dishes from the garden produce to conducting children's day camps in the summer months, from teach-ing courses in English as a second language to Venezuelan students to conducting seminars on etiquette for hotel receptionists, as well as teaching French to hotel employees on the island (I first learned about that responsibility just two days before the start of the course, by reading it in a newspaper ad!).

To top it all, we had started and were managing a youth hostel for young European travelers en route through Barbados to South America and then back again. This required a lot of work: registering new arrivals, sewing sheets for the bunk beds, laundering them, and all that goes with running a youth hostel.

The hardest work revolved around the hostel's bedding and laundry. Buying yards of purple sheeting material from a local fab-ric store, cut for me in the store into convenient six-foot lengths, and hemming the linens on my Singer treadle machine became a monthly occurrence, since my sheets regularly "disappeared." Of those that did not vanish, I laundered at least twenty of them daily. It was a never-ending job that no one else would do. Being as we did not own a washing machine, I used my feet to stomp the linens clean in an outdoor bathtub. Wringing out a batch of soapy water and then one of clear water from each sheet required throwing the drenched fabric over a washing line and twisting it against the line to squeeze out as much water as possible before hanging it evenly to dry in the tropical sun. The washing line was strung between two breadfruit trees.

Along with being the laundress for our guests, I was also the baker. Every evening, I kneaded twenty one-pound loaves of whole wheat bread. Dividing the twenty pounds of flour into two ten-pound batches and adding margarine, brewer's yeast, a little cane sugar, and warm water, I hand-mixed and kneaded the loaves and allowed them to rise before rekneading them to rise overnight for a second time in the oven in their individual one-pound pans, ready to bake early the next morning. These loaves provided not only breakfast for the youth hostelers, but also became a popular item for sale with our yoga students.

Oh, and did I mention that each Sunday afternoon I recorded daily episodes on yoga and related health topics for a daily women's program on a local radio station, for broadcasting during the next week? Amazing! I was busy morning, noon, and night.

The fact that I accomplished all these tasks as well as taught yoga classes and conducted yoga teacher training courses on top of a full-time job as a geography teacher in a government school seemed to encourage my husband to dream up more and more projects. In fact, he once told me in his imperious tone of voice, "It is for me to think up ideas, it is for others to work them out." In my moment of clarity and realization, I looked back in amazement at how I had accepted all this with little argument but with much inner anguish.

I had met Torrey at a meeting of the Baha'i spiritual community in Kensington, London. I was very attracted to his knowledge of different religions and his broad internationalism. A West Indian from

Barbados, he exuded charm and intelligence and presented an exotic perspective on life I felt I was missing in mine although I had searched for it. And here he was, available and delightful, with a charismatic personality. He was irresistible and I eloped with him soon after my twenty-first birthday. In retrospect, it was a foolhardy thing to do in many ways, but in other ways it was the making of me. My early marriage to Torrey was fun and lively, enriching my life by opening me up to friends from countless countries and cultures. It also produced a son, Owen, the quintessential child of mixed race who slips seamlessly from one identity to another with little friction. Yet, in the long run, the marriage was deeply flawed, disappointing and very frustrating.

My friends were amazed at my resilience and fortitude over the ten years we managed the Yoga Center. But Torrey's demand for me to sweep the yoga room at once was the last straw. Strong survival instincts surged through my whole being and found a voice, telling me to get out. It was like a glimmer of light in a long, dark tunnel. Although I was no longer in a concentration camp, it suddenly felt as though I was. This epiphany defined the end of my twenty-four-year marriage.

It is now 2009. I am seventy-two years old and look back on what seems to me now to be several different lifetimes in this one life. It has been a life with many twists and turns, yet each has built on the one before. Looking back at that first glimmer of light, after my first question, "Why?" in Barbados, subsequent questions came to me: "What did the concentration camp years teach me?", "How did they influence my adult choices and behaviors?" I had never asked those questions before. And now I ask myself, "How do they still affect me to this day, sixty years after the war is over?"

This is not a story of a failed marriage. Rather, it is a story of internal choice and consequence: mine. Not to choose is also a choice, as I came to realize. I was to embark on a search for meaning and purpose in my life, one that would give me more inner understanding. Why had I never questioned my choices? It did not seem necessary, as life on the whole was very good. I had a natural curiosity, which opened me up to many interesting adventures and experiences. I was always very busy and I occupied myself with fascinating projects, both in work as a teacher and in my personal life. Yet while my life seemed to roll along in an interesting fashion on the outside, my inner life was usually in turmoil. On the surface I looked very accomplished, yet I functioned at some deeply constrained level, unable to discuss any of my inner frustrations with anyone, especially concerning the years of my first marriage. A close friend of mine at that time said to me, "Phyllis, when you know who Phyllis is, you'll do amazing things. You are such a survivor." That really puzzled me. I was forty-three years old.

Yet I had lived through Japanese concentration camps with my mother and younger brother, Donald. I was a survivor, but mostly that was thanks to my mother in whose care I survived. Was I acting out in my adult years behaviors I had learned during those earlier formative years in concentration camps? I was completely unaware of the process of how I did things and why. I began to question my actions and motives. A pattern gradually emerged. Although I was very hardworking and accomplished, an underlying need to please and be obedient had become increasingly evident. My roller coaster of activities and constant learning were deeply linked to a need to suppress my own ideas in fear of what others would do to me if I did not accomplish what they wished. I also realized I had a suspicion of authority and used secrecy to get my way. In addition, I never freely said what was deeply on my mind, for fear of recrimination and punishment. I was so focused on achievement that I was oblivious to my actually being emotionally unavailable and submissive to other people. The sociable loner, I learned to be charming and helpful without actually allowing anyone to know me. I was determined to unlock the secrets of the past to free myself of these hidden prisons in my mind.

I did divorce Torrey in December 1981. Torrey did not contest it. In 1982, I moved to a new country, new job, and eventually remarriage. I transformed my life. It was a conscious act.

It came about like this: Some dear friends of mine in Barbados, Americans who owned a business on the island, came to me in December 1980 and asked me, "How would you like to teach yoga in Mexico?" I eagerly replied, "When?" I was born in Mexico, where my parents lived while my father was working for the Shell Oil Company in Tampico, so the connection was instantaneous. The door to Rancho la Puerta Fitness Resort and Spa in Tecate, Baja California, Mexico, was opened for me to enter in July 1981 as a guest instructor to teach yoga during the summer vacation.

It took over a year of paperwork to make the final transition to leave my job as a geography teacher, to tie off loose ends with the Yoga Center, to finalize the divorce, to make sure my eighteen-year-old son's education was completed for his career as a land surveyor, and to apply for a green card through my American mother living in Spain. Never burn your bridges, my father always taught me. I did my best to leave Barbados gracefully, and when I finally did my divorce lawyer told me that I would always be welcome back.

Soon, I was fortunate to obtain full-time work as a yoga and fitness instructor in this world-famous fitness resort and spa. My new life gave me space and time to reflect.

Living and working in the country of my birth felt right to me, as if I had come full circle. It was perfect. Within two years I was helping to organize the fitness department and eventually became fitness director, a position I held for eighteen years. Now I direct the "Spirit Week" and "Specialty Fitness Week" programs throughout the year for "the Ranch," as Rancho la Puerta is fondly referred to.

Gradually, answers came to me through reading, meeting people, contemplation, and meditation. The Ranch provides a wealthy source of information from visiting speakers. I opened up gradually to people I trusted. I quickly made many new friends. Evening lectures at the Ranch on post-traumatic stress disorder, handwriting analysis, dream interpretation, and much more were additional avenues to many ideas for me. I read war books and memoirs by other internees, the most valuable to me written by Laurens van der Post: "Venture to the Interior" and Victor Frankl: "Search for Meaning". I studied many philosophies, learned about the body-mind-spirit connection and psycho-neuroimmunology, and attended self-improvement courses and self-esteem conferences. My interest and practice of yoga and Vipassana meditation, a branch of Theravada Buddhism, as well as teaching Insight Meditation to Ranch guests in my "Inner Journey" program, to calm the mind and raise consciousness through mindfulness practices, continued in an atmosphere of spaciousness and freedom at Rancho la Puerta.

Time spent wondering why my life had been so difficult in my early adulthood brought realizations linking my behaviors to early concentration camp experiences. I realized that the behaviors and attitudes learned for survival at so young an age did not serve me well as an adult. I needed new behaviors, appropriate to being free and to freely exercising choice and accepting responsibility for the consequences. It was all frightening at first, yet with the potential to be very freeing.

I was caught in deeply ingrained patterns, especially those relating to authority. Nightmares gripped me ominously in my sleep, waking me in a vice of terror. You know the kind where you desperately run away from a dangerously aggressive maniac in menacing pursuit and you get nowhere, you try to scream, but the scream is a guttural croak gasping in the back of the throat, which eventually wakes you up in a sweat but thankful that it was only a dream. As I began to understand the forces that had shaped me, my nightmares gradually lessened, only to resurface very occasionally. Could I acknowledge those forces and move on? Old habits die hard, it is said. I began to recognize old gremlins lurking in the back of my mind—fears, doubts, and distrust of myself and sometimes of others in certain situations. I was particularly distrustful of people who used their power to control others, to be manipulative and authoritarian.

Even with my wonderful new job and happy productive life, the weekly border crossing between the United States and Mexico, especially the return into the former, bothered me a great deal in the early years at the Ranch, with flurries of nervousness flooding over me as I approached the border guards. The guards, holstered guns on their hips, would routinely bark questions in rapid, bullet like succession: "Where do you live?", "Why were you in Mexico?", "Is this your car?" (occasionally giving it a good kick), "Have you anything to declare?" The slightest hesitation in answering any one of them resulted in being pulled over and questioned further—and this was before 9/11. The sometime bullying, kicking my car (for what, I wondered?), and occasional harassment about my accent and nationality, although relatively infrequent episodes, were a continual cause of stress for me, as I anticipated such possibilities with dread. I mastered the American accent to avoid further questioning, answering, "Yep," "Nope," and "San Diego," drawing out the vowels in good American style. I listened to the calm reassurances of my second husband, Herb: "Relax, Phyllis, you are perfectly okay. Nothing will happen to you," and I even calmed myself with projections, picturing myself surrounded by white light. But it would be years before I would make the connection between this weekly ordeal and the fact that I had spent many years hiding my mother's precious American passport from Japanese prison guards by concealing it in my oversized underpants. But more of that later.

Through self-questioning, I attempted to reshape a new life within the boundaries of my work at the Ranch, creating a positive working environment, one based on cooperation and trust. My newfound position of responsibility gave me the opportunity to create a harmonious culture with my colleagues, one that could foster both professional and personal growth. I was gradually unraveling who I was and what had made me a survivor. My "peace at any cost" behaviors had not served me well over the years. Certain kinds of people who recognized it had often taken advantage of me, which had always been a difficult situation for me to confront. How could I retrain myself to resolve differences of opinion in a civilized way without conflict, yet without denying my own voice? While learning to create a peaceful environment, I attempted to surround myself with people of goodwill and peaceful intentions while exercising creativity, fun, and good energy. It was and still is a challenge. But this time, it is one of my choosing.

Yet, side by side with my positive experiences in my attempts to understand who I am, I also unleashed hidden terrors that I could not explain, especially those relating to authority: an inexplicable tightness in the chest when asked to do something by my boss or a feeling of fear of some unknown dimension. My next step was to get more in-depth information about the concentration camp years. Only my parents could give me that information from their adult memories of the war years.

The question of where I was born and where I had grown up frequently came up in conversation with Ranch guests. My English accent made it easy to give a short answer, depending on who asked. "I was brought up in England," I would reply. If I was asked where I was born and I replied, "Mexico," discerning questioners would probe deeper and there it was again, my childhood in Java and the concentration camp years. Everyone was always fascinated. I gave a general account of the four camps we were forced to live in. Short and sweet. I offered little detail and no emotion. My accounts were always cut and dried, matter of fact, and sometimes laced with humor.

I felt confused about some of the circumstances I had lived through in Java. Which memory came first? It didn't really matter to my listeners, but it began to matter to me. While I could remember some of the more dramatic experiences in the camps, I did not know the names of those camps or the order of many of those experiences. I was, after all, only five years old in Java at the start of the war after Pearl Harbor.

In 1983, I wrote to my mother, listing many questions about the war years, the camps, and the order of events I was trying to remember. My parents had retired to Spain in the early 1960s. I kept in touch with monthly phone calls and regular letters. But this letter went months without a reply. This was unusual. My mother is the family correspondent, keeping us all informed of one another's activities and adventures, a valuable international grapevine of family events. She is never at a loss for words. Other letters from her, giving family information, arrived without answering my questions. Her long silence to those questions intrigued me. Over the phone she told me, "Some of your questions are best answered by Daddy. But Daddy and I have never spoken about the war years to each other since the war, only to you two children when you asked. It is very difficult for your father and me to start now. That is why I have not answered your questions." I was amazed by this reply! But it was true. My parents had rarely talked about the war years while I grew up in England, only occasionally when Donald and I asked and certainly not in front of each other even when we were around. My father was now in his seventies and his eyesight was deteriorating, so he relied on my mother to write everything for him. I asked if she could at least answer the questions to which she alone could reply.

Six months later, I received a ninety-minute tape recording. My parents resolved the problem by telling their individual stories to their friends during the weekly bridge games they enjoyed together. Over a period of six months, the story gradually unfolded: my mother's story interspersed with my father's. This was the first time I had ever heard my father's experience. I was stunned. I wept. It did answer many of my questions. When my parents first told me their collective story, it was for the purpose of giving me more insight into that early experience of my life. My mother's story especially would give me greater knowledge of those years we shared in captivity. Many more questions surfaced over the following years and I saved them up for my visits with my parents whenever I could travel to Spain or they came to visit me at the Ranch.

While I still have my private memories of those frightening World War II years, the story I am about to tell you is of our experiences in Java before and during the war, predominantly as told to me by my parents forty and fifty years later. Much of this story is a woven fabric of my family's experiences, my mother's, my father's, my brother's, and mine, our collective memory that I share with you, my reader.

CHAPTER ONE

FAMILY

My Early Life in Java

I was five and a half years old when Japanese soldiers took my father away. My two-year-old brother, Donald, and I were standing at the front door beside our mother as we watched the military truck recede down the road. My father's face, along with the faces of other men packed in with him, looked back at us. He gave us a small wave. He disappeared into the night.

At the time, we were living in someone else's house, that of a Dutch family that had left the island and abandoned their home months earlier. My parents tried to keep our family as far from the Japanese troops as possible. Then the inevitable day came, when we had our first military encounter with Japanese soldiers. Until that evening, we were not really bothered by them at all. There was a noise outside and a knock at the door, and, when we opened it, a Japanese officer, accompanied by a little soldier with a rifle and bayonet, plus a third man, an interpreter, marched in. The officer unfurled a big sheet of paper and started reading names. He eventually came to my father's name, which my father acknowledged. The officer immediately pointed to my father and to the little soldier, indicating that the soldier should take his place beside my father and not leave his side. My father was told that he could take one suitcase with clothes for two or three days. The little soldier followed him as he went into the

15

bedroom to get these clothes. Everything was quite friendly up to that point, but as soon as he was taken away from the house and out into the garden, all friendliness disappeared. A bayonet was stuck in his back and he was marched to a large military truck that was standing at the gate.

Father: "*The soldier shoved the bayonet harder into my back to indicate that I should climb up. I hurriedly did so, joining a lot of fellows packed in there already. I was handcuffed to one of them. I felt terrible leaving my family like that, unprotected and on their own. I caught a last glimpse of them at the front door as we went off in the dark.*"

It would be three and a half years before I saw my father again. During that time, we never knew where he was located or if he was alive. He just "disappeared" along with all the other men.

WHAT BROUGHT US TO JAVA?

My father, a Scotsman, had first worked as a chemical engineer for the Shell Oil Company in Mexico. It was there he met and married my mother, an American, on September 25, 1935, and it was there I was born on August 1, 1936, in the refinery town of Tampico, on the coast of the Gulf of Mexico. In 1938, the Mexican government expropriated the oil companies in Mexico and my father was transferred to the Dutch East Indies. The Royal Dutch Shell and British Petroleum Company combined to run a very big paraffin wax plant in Balikpapan, in Borneo, and as he had experience in wax manufacture, that was where he was sent. Paraffin wax was in great demand for the batik industry in that part of the world. After a year in Borneo, my father was transferred to Java, where we spent the next two years. He worked in the refinery in Tjepoe.

Tjepoe (or Cepu, as it is known today) is a small community on the northeast coast of Java. Surrounded by small villages, it was a refinery town with a housing estate where the refinery workers lived. The estate included a club with a swimming pool, a golf course, and a little kindergarten that I attended. My brother, Donald, was born in Tjepoe on July 4, 1939. We lived in quite a large house with a nice garden around it, near the edge of a big teak forest. We had five servants: the "number one boy"; the "number two boy"; the cook known as "the cookie"; the "babu," who was my and my brother's nursemaid; and the "dogsbody" who did all the jobs the other four wouldn't do.

Dorothy Nisbet with first born Phyllis, 1936

Mother, Dorothy Nisbet, Phyllis, and Father, Frank Nisbet, in their garden

Phyllis with her father in their garden

Phyllis' first Birthday, with nanny

On Sundays, we often went for rides into the teak forest right in the center of the jungle. We would stop the car and sit very quietly and watch all the wildlife come out: the monkeys, wild pigs, wild peacocks, and various other creatures. The monkeys in Java were very small, and their little babies clung to the chests of the mothers. These little babies were only about as long as my little fingers, with absolutely no fur on them at all, and had little tiny pinpoint black eyes. The mothers would swing from branch to branch with the babies still hanging onto them. I loved those rides into the jungle with its troops of monkeys, and seeing all the different animals and birds. My mother would point them out to me as we sat quietly in the car.

When we'd lived in Borneo, the monkeys that came down from the jungle were orangutans. The troop would gather in the cashew trees around our house. The top branch of one of those trees was level with the window of my bedroom. According to my mother, who would dress and wash me and comb my hair and tie it in ribbons each morning, all the mama orangutans would sit on the branches of the tree with their babies on their laps, chattering to one another and carrying on—as if to say, "What on earth is that woman doing to that child in there?" They never attempted to come in the room, although the windows were wide open. We had a lot of fun watching them, and they had a lot of fun watching us.

Pleasant vignettes of my early life in Java run through my memory: playing in our spacious garden with my brother, running down the lane to meet my father when he returned from work on his bicycle, riding back with him on the backseat of his bicycle with my legs outstretched, or riding in a horse and buggy to and from the company swimming pool. The house we lived in was built on stilts and surrounded by beautiful shade trees. We often played in the garden in the care of our babu, the young Javanese girl who helped to look after us during the day.

My mother Dorothy, a petite woman with curly dark hair and a lovely smile, loved to visit the local markets and often took me along with her. The local communities were not far from where we lived. Visiting the Chinese market to pick up spices, I would look out for the old man with the long thumbnail encased in an ornately engraved sheath. The nail and its sheath must have been at least two inches long and he displayed it prominently by arranging his hands in his lap. "Why does he have such a long nail and cover it like that?" I asked my mother. "It indicates his privileged position in society and shows that he does not need to work with his hands," she replied.

Family home in Balakpapan, Borneo, 1938

Phyllis with passenger on board to the Dutch East Indies

Phyllis with father at Balakpapan Airport

Phyllis on the steps of their house

My mother got along very well with the Chinese community, which was known as the "Kong." They made all our clothes and provided us with her favorite Chinese foods. She strongly believed in eating "local," as she called it. Occasionally, she took a parcel along to them as a gift. Red Cross supplies from the United States were available to her because she was an American citizen. When members of the Kong fell ill, she would bring them medicine sent to her by the Red Cross.

My father taught golf to some of the Javanese men who caddied at the golf course. It seemed as if my parents endeared themselves to many members of the Chinese and local community. The head of the Kong told my mother repeatedly to let him know any time she was in need of anything, that someone in the community would provide it for her (little did we know the extent to which this promise would be fulfilled many years later).

Accompanying my mother on her shopping trips was always an exciting adventure for me. The colorful markets exuded the exotic smells of curry powders, cinnamon, and cardamom, along with the smell of fried foods and the fragrant scents of ripe tropical fruits: mangoes, papayas, lychees, and so many more.

Brilliant batik fabrics draped many of the stalls. The sounds of bartering as people shopped, along with the occasional stringed musical instrument accompanying a lovely song enveloped my senses. Somehow that sense of community seeped into my young consciousness, a wordless communication through deed.

A TJEPOE BIRTHDAY

My fifth birthday party was filled with fun and games. It was held in the garden of our house. A big wicker chair decorated with hibiscus flowers was mine for the day and stood grandly at one end of the garden. It was a Dutch custom in the Dutch East Indies to decorate the birthday chair. On that day, ornately entwined leaves, brilliant red hibiscus flowers, and orchids decorated the back rim of my appointed chair. Tables laden with sandwiches, cakes, and fruits lined the grass to one side of the garden, while the spacious lawn provided room for games in the shade of the trees.

The highlight of the afternoon was a piñata hanging by a cord from a tree branch. Blindfolded, each of my young friends took turns cracking open the piñata, using one of my father's golf clubs. I can still feel the thrill of being spun around and trying to guess where to hit, missing over and over to the accompaniment of gales of laughter. An older girl finally whacked the piñata free, spilling its candies over the grass to be descended upon by a mass of scrambling children.

Several months after my birthday, our tranquil life changed. My mother, brother, and I left for the mountains. We were sent up to the hill station called Sarangan, along with the Dutch women and all the children from the company's housing estate. We were kept there supposedly in safety until such time when the Dutch figured out what was going to happen to us. My father did not come with us. He had to stay behind to manage the refinery.

Phyllis and Donald on donkeys, and two locals, Sarangan, 1940

As my father tells it: *"Life in Java went on quite normally until Pearl Harbor in December of '41, after which the Japanese invaded countries south of Japan. Various places were falling into Japanese hands, including Hong Kong, Malaya, and Singapore. Before that year was out, the Japanese swept down the Asian coast in a matter of weeks and occupied Java, along with the other islands then known as the Dutch East Indies. Many families had left for Australia, sensing the imminent danger. Two British battleships were sunk. Things began to look very serious. All the Dutch 'technologs,' that is, men with university degrees, were reserve officers in the Dutch army and were called up. Those who were not in the army were put into the reserve or, as we would call it in Britain, the Home Guard. I was the only European left to run the refinery, with the help of the native staff."*

My father, on his own, carried on operating the refinery as usual until the day the Japanese landed. The Dutch had made arrangement to blow up the refinery and all the tanks around the house. But they forgot to tell my father about it. He remembers: *"I awoke one morning to reverberating explosions of oil tanks. Planes were flying pretty close to the house and dropping their bombs on the refinery. They were Dutch planes enacting their 'scorched-earth policy' and blowing up their own refinery. This policy of destruction was to prevent anything useful to fall into Japanese hands. I hurriedly got dressed, sought out the head cook, and told him that I was getting out. He agreed that that was the only thing to do. But I was on the lowlands and all of my family was up in the mountains. I set off in our old car, but when I got to the bottom of the hill leading up to Sarangan, the very steep mountain road was too much for it. I got about halfway up and the old car just wouldn't take it anymore, so I had to get out and walk the rest of the way. I left the car and got some native boys to carry the stuff in it up to the village where I met all of you."*

My father told us that he thought there was some chance of getting out at Tjilatjap (now called Cilacap), a port on the south coast. If we could reach there by crossing the mountain, we might get a boat out of Java. We gathered up all our things and kept the two young men that were carrying the belongings Daddy had taken from the car. My parents decided to bring everything we possessed back to the vehicle. When we reached it, however, we found that our car, too, had been burned to the ground on the Dutch government's "scorched-earth policy." The boys were very helpful and managed to find two donkeys for us. Donald and I shared one donkey, and what baggage we had was put on the other. My mother and father walked beside us. We walked right over the mountain and down to a town on the hillside, where we met some Swiss people who put us up overnight.

My mother recalls that one of the bags she had taken up to the hill station with her was a wardrobe trunk. It had all our valuables in it: things she had bought in Java, all the silver my father had won in golf tournaments in both Mexico and Java, all their amber and crystal wedding presents from Mexico, and their Delphi china. All these things were packed in the trunk with clothes wrapped around them to keep them safe. We left the trunk with all these valuables with the Swiss people who said they'd take care of it for us until after the war. (At the end of the war, my parents contacted them for their belongings, but they claimed ignorance of ever having them and said they had nothing of ours—so everything was lost!)

At vast expense, my father hired a taxi, which was willing to take us to Solo, a town halfway down to the coast. The taxi only had five liters of gasoline so it had to freewheel practically all the way down the mountainside, but it eventually got us to Solo, where we picked up a train to take us to Tjilatjap. About fifteen minutes before the train arrived at Solo, it had been strafed by machine-gun fire from Japanese planes and the roof was full of bullet holes. But it did arrive safely, albeit with some injured passengers. The carriages were jam-packed with people, and more were hanging on the sides. We managed to squeeze into the train and eventually got to Tjilatjap.

There had been a lot of ships in port loaded with people trying to escape from Java. The day before we arrived, the Japanese had bombed the whole port, sinking every one of those vessels. The ship that was to carry us to safety had been commandeered as a troop ship by the Dutch government. It was in a sense fortuitous that we did not board it, because the Japanese bombed and sank that, too. Many of the survivors were returned to Java later as prisoners of war. Ironically, they joined us in the camps. In the end, there wasn't a single ship that escaped from Tjilatjap. We managed to find a little hotel in the bombed city and moved in.

The people who had gone on the ships left masses of cars on the docks, so after settling into the hotel my father went and looked around the docks to find a car that would work. He found one that had the keys in it; unfortunately, it had no gasoline. He knew a British antiaircraft battalion was in Tjilatjap, fighting the Japanese planes. We all went over and he asked the commander if we could have some gasoline, which he very kindly provided. Our only option was to get out of Tjilatjap and go up to Bandoeng (now called Bandung), where the Shell Oil Company offices were headquartered, but it was impossible to leave Tjilatjap immediately because the Japanese were bombing and strafing the town 24 hours a day with aerial machine-gun fire.

We spent the first day in an air-raid shelter with masses of people. It was a huge underground space with a curved ceiling with lights glowing from it. We entered down some steps and then huddled inside with hundreds of people. I did not like that one little bit and neither did my mother, who did not consider it a safe place for us. She flatly refused to go back in it the next day, so we spent our time under the bed in the hotel, which she considered a lot safer. She was proved right on that one, because the next day a bomb went clean through the whole air-raid shelter and wiped everybody out.

THE TASTE OF WHITE RUBBER

While my parents, Donald, and I spent a couple of days hiding under the bed, a very enterprising young gentleman called Lieutenant Hunt turned up. He was enlisted with a British military operation. He had come down Indochina all the way through Malaysia, laying booby traps for the Japanese. He was on their blacklist and wanted out in a hurry. It was his intention to get to Australia, but he couldn't get out of Tjilatjap any more than the rest of us could.

The frequent air raids and bomb blasts were very loud and frightening and seemed very near. Everything in the room rattled and shook. We hid under the bed every time there was an air raid, biting on a piece of raw rubber that Lieutenant Hunt had given each of us. He had a pocket full of the flat squares, collected from the rubber plantations in Malaya. He said to us, "Here, bite on this, it will stop your teeth from rattling when the bombs drop." The taste of that white rubber stays with me to this day. I have only to see the creamy colored crepe rubber on the soles of shoes in shop windows to remind me of those scary days we spent under the bed biting on flat chunks of raw rubber. As my mother describes those days in the hotel with Lieutenant Hunt: *"Lieutenant Hunt was an enterprising young man, trim in his uniform, slim built, and energetic. He told us many a story of how he foiled the Japanese from traveling down the peninsula of Malaya. Much of what he did was quite dangerous. Exploring the hotel, Lieutenant Hunt found a champagne cellar in the basement, which nobody else knew anything about. He only told Daddy and me about it, and the five of us—that was Daddy, you, Donald, Mr. Hunt, and me—spent our time in the champagne cellar for the next four days. As the air raids went on, we used up quite a bit of the champagne! Of course, you two children did not drink any, but we had some nice parties down there as the bombs dropped around us. Eventually, the air raids stopped and Lieutenant Hunt left in a dhow, a local sailing boat, with some natives, to try to get to Australia. He tried to persuade us to go with him, but with you two children in tow we felt it was too risky. We never did hear from him again, but we hoped he would get to Australia safely."*

THE JOURNEY TO BANDOENG

Mother: *"Instead, the four of us—Daddy, you two, and I—went off in the car to try to get up to Bandoeng. Our main problem was that we couldn't get any food to take with us before we left, so we had to take off on a several-hundred-mile journey west across the island without food or water. We just had to hope that we could gather something on the way. We were strafed by airplanes several times and had to stop the car and hide in banana plantations growing alongside the road. On occasion, when there was nowhere to hide we had to dive into a flooded rice field to dodge bombs and bullets that were falling around us. Wearing coolie hats to protect us from the sun, and also to act as camouflage, we submerged ourselves into the paddy fields with just our noses sticking out for air. Fortunately, the car was not hit and neither were we, and we managed to keep going.*

"On one of the mountain passes, we happened to come across a British air force battalion going in the opposite direction. We stopped

them and asked if they had any food they could give to you two children.
They very kindly stopped the whole battalion of men and created
a picnic right there with their beef and biscuits and army rations.
They gave us some food to take with us and sent us on our way, along
with some extra gallons of gasoline and water. Eventually we arrived
in Bandoeng.

"We happened to meet the man in charge of that battalion many
years after the war was finished; he was working for the Shell Oil Com-
pany and we were quite surprised to find each other again."

My own memory of the journey inland over the mountains is
a vague blend of luscious banana plantations on one side of the dirt
road, with spacious open paddy fields on the other. As we climbed
higher inland from the coast, beautiful panoramic mountain scenes
converged with occasional air battles. One time, two airplanes, both
Japanese and bearing the sign of the "Rising Sun", crashed into each
other. We watched the whole scene to the cheers of my parents as the
aircraft nose-dived in flames into the jungle, trailing smoke.

The mountain ridges along our journey became more spectacu-
lar. A bomb-damaged hotel whose front balcony was hanging down
provided us with a place to spend one of the nights. As I submerged
my body into hot water in our room's bathtub that evening, the contact produced a strange tingle of comfort rippling over my skin, pro-
ducing a sense of well-being and security. My mother told me the
hotel was undoubtedly European: it was unusual in Java, wartime
notwithstanding, to bathe in hot water in a white-enameled bathtub. The typical Javanese bath consisted of an open concrete tank of
cold water equipped with a coconut shell on a handle to ladle water.

Perhaps it is not so strange that the feeling of comfort and safety I felt in the hot water bath recurs to this day. I love warm baths and take them frequently after a day's work, sometimes musing on the body's memory of events so long ago. My need for warm baths, for soaking in the safety of my present life, still gives me time to pause, reflect, and evaluate where I am. It took me years to pinpoint the source of this powerful sensation, tracing it back to the mountain haven and a brief moment of comfort during those dangerous times.

Blue Pudding in Bandoeng

We finally arrived in Bandoeng. As my father recalls: *"We didn't get a very great welcome from any Dutch people we contacted. In fact, we couldn't get anywhere to sleep that night. We hunted around the town. Eventually we found a little boardinghouse that was being run by a German woman. She gave up her own bed for your mother and you two children. She ran this little boardinghouse 'Box and Cox' style, mainly for Dutch sailors.* [My father was fond of quoting famous tales, "Box and Cox" being one of them: Box sleeping by day and Cox by night so that the landlady could earn two sums of money from one room.] *"The following day we managed to get into the finest and biggest hotel in town—the Preanger Hotel. I finally located the house where the Shell people had set up an office. They gave me some money and told me I was just in time to get a ship leaving the following day and that I could go out on it. I said, 'Oh good, I'll go and collect my wife and children.' 'No,' they said, 'No women and children, only men are going.' So I refused to go, but all the Dutch men went on it, leaving their families behind.*

"As a matter of fact, the ship was sunk and most of the men were lost at sea. There were six of them saved and they were prisoners in Sumatra. Two of them died in camp. One of the survivors was Mr. Olsen, the Shell director in Java."

My mother says of her experience in the hotel: "*The fine hotel was full of Dutch people who were also fleeing from the Japanese, along with a Frenchwoman and her husband. The French lady and I helped in the kitchen, where two Australian soldiers did all the cooking. We helped out a bit with chopping and preparing, and did all the serving after the food was cooked. They did all the cleaning and washing up afterward. We waited hand and foot on all these Dutch people who were sitting in the dining room expecting to be catered to. None of them would have eaten if it weren't for the Australian soldiers, the French lady, and me. The two Australian soldiers were AWOL. They'd run away from their regiment. They were really good fun. They found huge tins of corned beef but we couldn't find a tin opener anywhere. So they found a hatchet out back and used it to open the tins.*

"*The Japanese finally came. We were in the best hotel in Bandoeng, so they commandeered it and turned out all the Dutch people. They kept the two Australians, the French lady and me, Daddy, and you two children, but we still wound up cooking for them. In fact, they ordered us to cook for them. We did this for about three days, until they brought in their own Japanese cooks. On the second day, one of the high-ranking Japanese officers celebrated his birthday and ordered a blue pudding for his birthday party. So the orders came out to the kitchen... blue pudding. We asked the two Australians, 'How do you make a blue pudding?' 'Leave it to us, ladies, leave it to us, we'll do it.' So the*

French lady and I left them to it. They produced a beautiful big blue pudding, a blancmange of the most electric blue you have ever seen. The color was very startling. In astonishment we asked, 'What did you color it with?' 'Rickets Blue, ladies, Rickets Blue!' That's the stuff you wash whites with to make them whiter. They found a packet of it in the kitchen, and used it to color a white blancmange. The party was a great success and the officer seemed well satisfied with his birthday pudding. Fortunately for us, the officers experienced no ill effects afterward!"

While my mother was working in the kitchen, my father was left to look after my brother and me. We had fun playing games and telling stories. On one of the days, what few clothes we had with us needed washing. My father took charge of the situation. He put all the clothes into the bathtub, added soap and water, and put the two of us in to stomp on the clothes. We had the best fun, splashing and laughing, and then did it all over again with clean water. My father wrung out the clothes on the line in the garden and then hung them up to dry. Since my father had never done the washing before, my mother was suitably impressed and told him he did a smashing job.

Mother: *"Once the Japanese knew their cooks were on the way, they gave us 24-hours' notice to leave the hotel, it so happened the day before we were told to leave. Daddy was in town and met Vena. Now, Vena was a very good friend of ours whom we had met in Borneo—a petite, very pretty, dark-haired Englishwoman who was married to a Dutch man called Martin Versloet. He was a doctor practicing in Borneo. She had a son, Ron, who was a couple of months younger than Donald. Vena and Martin had been in Java on holiday from Balikpapan, in Borneo, when Pearl Harbor happened, and they didn't* go back to Borneo, which was just as well because all the men who were at Balikpapan had an escape route worked out through the jungle. The plan began with leading the men to a little village where they had prepared a hut with food, water, and clothes and things to use for the remainder of their escape. The Japanese met them there and shut them all up into a shed and set the shed on fire. All the men were killed. That would have been Martin's fate if he had been there. Vena and Martin had rented a little house in Bandoeng just a few days before we met Vena. Martin had been called up by the military as a liaison officer between the Dutch and the British, so Vena was on her own in this little house. She immediately said we should come and join her. We left the hotel the next day and went up to the house Vena had rented and joined her and Ron there."

Father: "When the Japanese army took over in Bandoeng, the first thing they did was to round up all the Dutch soldiers and put them into a camp. Vena and I did manage to go and see Martin who was in the camp. While there, I saw another young Dutch man who I worked with in Tjepoe. This young Dutch man was a reserve officer in the army and he had been stationed at the coast when the Japanese landed close to the refinery in Tjepoe. His unit eventually arrived in Bandoeng. He had never seen a Japanese soldier until he was put into the camp in Bandoeng."

Mother: "For some reason, Vena hadn't been living in this little rented house for a couple of weeks, accompanying Martin perhaps. While she had been away, the Japanese soldiers had moved in, wrecked it, and left. You never saw such a mess in a house as we found when we went there with her. The Japanese had used everything in the house for

toilets, except the toilets. They had broken everything that was break-
able except the solid furniture, and it took Vena and me a week to get
the place clean. All the locks were broken on the doors, but we felt safe
enough with your father in the house and that didn't worry us—until
he was picked up."

WITHOUT MY FATHER

After my father left in the truck with the Japanese soldiers, I remember my mother and Auntie Vena discussing our new situation, concerned about our safety and living unprotected. I cannot remember much of this time except my mother's anxiety and the busyness that followed. Not feeling safe in the house without locks after my father was taken away, my mother and Auntie Vena decided to move to a different house. We had very few possessions and clothes, so moving didn't seem to create many problems. Our one suitcase was ready to go.

Many years later, when I asked my mother how she felt as my father was taken away, she replied, *"Abandoned—I felt abandoned again."* I asked her, "Why 'again'?" which brought back deep memories of growing up in Hawaii, being left by her mother when she was five years old and further abandoned by her traveling-salesman father who had put her in a Catholic boarding school, run by French nuns in Honolulu, until she was eighteen.

My mother remembers: *"Without Frank, I was left with a terrible empty feeling. The pit of my stomach felt as if it had dropped out of me. I felt unprotected and vulnerable. Vena and I wanted a house with locks. We explored the neighborhood and heard of a house that was empty two or three blocks away and moved into it. It was a large house built near the top of a hill on a wide avenue lined with trees, in what was once an upscale residential area. In addition, the view from the spacious back porch overlooking the mountains was magnificent, with carefully tended terraced slopes, paddy fields in the valleys, and forested ridges overlapping each other into misty distances. It was very private from outsiders and a perfect haven for us.*

"Although it had four bedrooms, we moved enough beds into one bedroom for the five of us to sleep in. To make sure that nobody was going to attack us while we were asleep, we filled a flit-gun with ground-up red hot peppers and vinegar and placed the weights from the kitchen scales in the toes of socks and lined them up behind the door. If anybody came to the door, we had it worked out that Vena was going to squirt them in the face with the vinegar and red hot peppers and I would bash them over the head with the weights. And that would take care of anybody who dared to try and attack us. It so happened that someone did try to break in once, but we had a little dog that barked like mad and the person went away."

The house with the beautiful mountain views was on an avenue lined with tall trees leading past the front door. The back of the house had a large patio and garden overlooking the mountains. Donald, Ron, and I ran around the neighborhood quite freely. We lived near the top of a hill surrounded by fine homes and gardens. A huge Great Dane dog in a neighbor's garden once barked ferociously at us while we played near their front gate. My brother and I clutched at each other in fear at its size and sound, then turned and ran back to the safety of "our" house. But other than this, it seemed a fairly peaceful time for us for several weeks, living in that big house on a hill with a beautiful view. Auntie Vena would take us for nature walks, teaching us to identify the various flowers. Bougainvillea, oleander, and hibiscus were abundant and colorful (I was unable to say hibiscus properly, and my mother tells me I called them "his biscuits.") Auntie Vena was quite the gardener, and among other quick-growing vegetables that she planted, such as lettuce and radishes, she also attempted to grow corn. But we were never to harvest her crop.

Mother: "*One day, a big car drove up outside the house with a Japanese officer, an interpreter, and an entourage of women beautifully dressed in elaborate kimonos. The women all lined up, bowing profusely and deeply to the officer as he passed them. The interpreter told us that this Japanese officer was a very famous painter in Japan. He also was some relation to the royal family and he wanted permission to paint the view from the house. Well, naturally we gave him permission. We didn't have much option. He was there for almost a month, painting the view from our back patio. The other Japanese in the neighborhood left us strictly alone during this time. It was clear our guest was a very high-ranking officer. When he left, he gave us a piece of paper with some Japanese writing on it to put on the door. He didn't tell us what was written on it, but said we had to pin this on the door. Two or three days later, Vena and I were out for a walk with you three children and met an Indonesian friend who had gone to ask for work from the Japanese. He told us that they had given him an armband to wear and that ever since then Japanese soldiers were following him all over the town and getting very angry with him. He couldn't understand why he was being accosted and verbally abused in this way until a friend who could read Japanese told him that the writing on his armband stated that he could take them to the best whorehouse in town. Well, Vena and I took one look at each other, said good-bye in a hurry, and raced back to the house, where we tore the paper off the door. It wasn't until years afterward that we found out what it said: that we were good women and that no Japanese soldier was to disturb us. We were together in the house for about six weeks, when a big truck arrived with about eighteen Japanese soldiers, complete with guns and bayonets, who came in and said that my two children and I were to come with them. I was to take what I could carry. I took our one suitcase, which was all I could manage, and you, Donald, and I got into the truck. Vena and Ron were left in the house alone. We were actually the first ones to be picked up, so we had eighteen soldiers and eighteen bayonets all to ourselves for a while. This time it was us waving good-bye to Aunty Vena and Ron from the back of our truck. Many stops later, our truck filled up with a dozen or so British women and their children the Japanese picked up along the way. We were taken to Kleina Lengkong Concentration Camp."*

CHAPTER TWO

CHALLENGE

KLEINA LENGKONG
CONCENTRATION CAMP

While we were in the truck, my mother quietly slipped her American passport into the back of the frilly bloomers beneath my dress. They were the kind with elastic around the legs, so the passport would not fall through. She told me to keep my hands away from my bottom and to never admit the passport was there, not even to Aunty Vena. I was absolutely forbidden to tell anybody. When we arrived at the camp gates, I jumped off the truck with my mother's help and, with her secret well hidden, I walked through the wide open gates into our first concentration camp. We were confronted with a wooden wall with high barbed-wire fencing, big gates opened wide allowing us all to pass through into a large yard with a building in the middle, and men with bayonets on either side of the main gate. I was swinging my arms confidently as I walked though those gates, mindful of my mother's admonition that I not touch the seat of my panties.

The Japanese had taken all the passports, all the wedding rings, and any other jewelry the women had. In later years, my mother explained to me that she was bound and determined that although the Japanese could have her jewelry if they wanted, and even her wedding ring, she certainly was not going to let them have her American passport. During the war, in all the various camps we were in, searches were regular occurrences. Whenever they made a search, mother put me into those bloomers—the only ones I owned with elastic in the legs—and hid her passport there. I didn't wear them all the time because she didn't want them to wear out. Fortunately, I never grew out of them during those camp years, due to our starvation diet, and the passport was never found!

What is very strange to me now is the fact that I remember only the very first time this happened, including the feeling of confidence I had felt while keeping this secret between my mother and myself as I walked through the gates of that first camp. Although we had dozens of inspections, or tenkos (tenko is the word for "counting" in Japanese) over the next three and half years in four different camps, I do not recall any of the subsequent times the passport was placed in my bloomers, although my mother assures me it was placed there every time. Was the danger of it being found too great for me to process? My mother would most certainly have been severely punished if ever it were found. My mother's insistence that I was carrying a "secret" known only to the two of us may have triggered a kind of partial amnesia that persists to this day.

I cannot even begin to think about all the ways in which it has affected my life over the years. I know I have always experienced an inner tension when asked by anyone to keep a secret. And I know I often manifest tension by an ache in my lower back, right where the passport would have lodged. During the entire time I spent in the camps, the mere existence of the passport was something too dangerous to acknowledge; but now, through meditation and conscious compassion, I try to reach out to the five-year-old self still residing in my body and psyche.

Kleina Lengkong Prison Camp had been a school for native children and was merely a series of little atap buildings with thatched roofs. Atap is a kind of hay or straw put on a roof, held up by four iron poles at the corners. Even the walls were made of flimsy atap weavings, to give some semblance of privacy between the rooms. Our building certainly wasn't a solid structure, as we think of buildings. Our new accommodations consisted of two rooms for us to sleep in, each about twenty-five feet square with cement floors; another smaller room that served as an office for the natives in charge of us; and an even smaller lean-to space without an enclosing atap wall, to be used as a hospital. In fact, the hospital portion was more like an outdoor area with merely a tilted roof over it.

We were crowded into our two allotted rooms with other women and children. After a lot of ordering around, we found ourselves in one of the rooms to be shared with many others packed in with us. My mother, brother and I managed to find some floor space just big enough for us to lie down on in the corner of one of the two rooms, next to the woven straw wall. We slept on the bare concrete at first, until my mother could buy some straw atap mats much like straw mats used on the beach today. Our one suitcase with all our belongings sat in the corner of our space.

A small room off to one side served as the toilet: a hole in the ground with hollowed footprints on either side to place your feet. There was very little privacy, considering the flimsiness of the atap walls and door. This toilet arrangement was totally inadequate, because it had to serve all of us women and children. A bucket, filled with water from a nearby tap was used to slush down the contents after each use. Often there was not enough water to go around. The hole was much too wide for many of the smaller children. My little brother, Donald, had to perch on the edge of one side to use it. One child fell in and had to be rescued, fortunately none the worse for the experience.

Mother: *"There were approximately eighty of us women and children in this camp; all British except me, the only American, occupying two rooms. The amount of space we had was exactly twenty-two inches wide by six feet long per person, and we were packed in like sardines in a tin and slept on a cement floor. The only staff members in charge of us, selected by the Japanese, were Javanese—two men and a woman. The two men didn't bother us at all and really had very little to do with us. But the woman was pretty awful—threw her weight around and made life as miserable as possible. She probably relished the reversal of roles between herself and a bunch of Western women. We were able to buy food at that time, so we got extra food over and above our rations.*

"During the first few months we were able to buy some sanitary protection for our menstrual cycles, but eventually we had to re-use the fabric after rinsing them out in order to maintain supplies. After eight months or so most of the woman stopped menstruating due to our increasingly meager rations, which solved that problem. There was an open fire at the back of the cement path, where we could do a bit of cooking. The first day we were there, the Japanese brought some rice, meat, and vegetables expecting it to feed all eighty of us, leaving it at the entrance of the camp for us to share. It was clear that the food would not divide easily into eighty equal portions. For some reason the women thought I would know how to divide this food and asked

me how to do it! I took one look and suggested that it be cooked as one large stew and we each get a share of the collective effort. So that is what we did. As none of us had ever cooked before in our privileged lives, we threw everything into one big pot with some water and hoped for the best. It turned out reasonably well and was fairly palatable. Cooking communally, we took turns at making these daily stews. In the early days, those of us with some money could buy milk for the children and a few eggs."

Three days after we first arrived in this camp, Auntie Vena and Ron joined us. Space was at a premium, but somehow they were squeezed into one of the two rooms along with the rest of us.

During the first week in this camp, I became aware of a very pretty woman hanging around the main gate. She had red hair and wore a tightly fitting green skirt with a black lacy knit top. She looked very different from all the other women and behaved very differently, too. When I next saw the lacily dressed woman standing by the main gate, I told my mother I thought she looked pretty and asked why she was dressed so differently. "She is being nice to the Japanese commandant, and hopes to get favors in return," was my mother's reply. I was left to wonder what that meant, but never asked for further details. My mother certainly did not offer them. As the pretty lady soon disappeared from the camp, I had no further reason to ask questions.

Mother: *"All of the women were very aware of the motivation of the Irish girl with the flaming red hair. She dressed herself very seductively. I was intrigued with the open knit of her tops, which showed her bare skin but still managed to cover her in the right places. She made herself up with such cosmetics as she had, to look attractive, and hung around the main gate every time the Japanese commandant showed up for his daily inspection of the camp. After one week in the camp, she disappeared, presumably successful in her plan to live more comfortably outside than inside. After we spent two or three months in this camp, a Japanese officer brought an attractive, well-dressed Australian woman to the camp in a fine car. It transpired that she was being 'punished' for somehow displeasing him, and he thought it a good idea for her to 'cool her heels' in the camp, to teach her a lesson. She was very quiet and spoke little to us of her decision to live with a Japanese officer. After three days, however, he returned in his fine car to retrieve her and we never saw her again. We never saw the Irish woman again, either, throughout the years of the war."*

A DIFFERENT SORT OF BIRTHDAY

I celebrated my sixth birthday in this camp, a memorable occasion. The women organized the party for the afternoon of my birthday, August 1, 1942. I cannot remember what food was served, but a big ceremony was organized, where I was to be dressed like a queen. A little boy my age played the part of a king. Whether it was his birthday as well is not clear to me now. Each wearing a crown made out of paper on our head, and sheets draped over our shoulders to create a long train held up by several other children, he and I paraded around the yard. Everyone sang "Happy Birthday" and also the Dutch version of that song, "Lang Zal Ze Leven" as we walked around in a stately manner. In the Dutch custom, two chairs decorated with flowers for the birthday celebrants stood grandly at the end of the yard. The boy and I were led ceremoniously to them. When we sat down in the chair we were both soaked to the skin, water splashing all around us. We both jumped up to gales of laughter from all around. They had disguised the seat of the chair with a fancy cloth covering a potty full of water. I recall the unpleasant feeling of being the brunt of everyone's joke... and on my birthday, too! How different from my fifth birthday, celebrated in our lovely garden in Tjepoe a year before with a piñata and delicious food. My six-year-old sensibilities were unable to grasp the humor played at my expense. I was very upset. Not even the hibiscus flowers around the chair could make up for the indignity I had experienced in that wet moment, a sharp contrast to the feeling of being admired as a queen during the grand parade around the yard. Nevertheless, I soon dried off in the tropical sun, the indignity soon forgotten, and enjoyed the rest of the festivities—games of tag and hide-and-seek, and a sing-along of nursery rhymes and popular children's songs of the day. Shortly after my birthday, my mother embroidered a handkerchief with the names of all the children in the camp. I possess it to this day, along with another handkerchief my mother embroidered with the names of all the women in that camp. The adults had chores given to them by the guards, which included sorting out the food delivered to the front gate daily, cooking it for everyone to share, keeping the camp clean with a broom and maybe a bucket of water, as well as making sure the toilet worked. This was always a dirty and foul-smelling job, which the women took turns to do. When they had any spare time, many women occupied themselves with sewing and mending whatever clothing they had and also embroidering and crocheting pretty little items such as pin-cushions, needle holders, and little bags to hold buttons and handkerchiefs.

The Women

*Hand-embroidered handkerchief with the names of the women imprisoned
in Kleina Lengkong Japanese Concentration Camp, Bandoeng/Java*

Hand-embroidered handkerchief with the names of the children imprisoned in Kleina Lengkong Japanese Concentration Camp, Bandoeng/Java

For me, the days there passed in the daily round of getting enough to eat and playing. We children had all sorts of ways to keep occupied. We jumped rope, told stories, and collected colorful bottle tops. Inside the metal caps of the milk bottles were painted pictures of different scenes and people in action. We valued those bottle tops and jealously guarded them from one another. My brother and I built quite a big collection in the several months our mother was able to buy milk and food from local traders who came to the camp gates. These special caps were such a big item that, when one child dropped a bottle top down the toilet hole his mother gallantly fished down in the hole—what a mess!—with her arm fully immersed, to rescue the treasure. She issued a warning to never lose it down there again, or it would stay there.

DONALD'S INJURY, MOTHER'S ILLNESS

Donald was only two years old, but he was always up to some mischief—climbing up onto things, always on the go. When he fell off a wall, gashing his head on the concrete ground, there was a huge commotion among the women. They lifted him off the ground as blood poured down his face. He had a deep cut on his forehead and was unconscious. The next thing I knew, Donald was whisked out of the camp by a Japanese guard. It all happened so quickly, even before my mother knew about it. I remained motionless as the women ran frantically around, calling out my mother's name, "Dorothy, Dorothy," to tell her of the accident and that her son had been removed from the camp. Just how I felt at that time is not really clear to me now. Looking back on it, the only explanation I can give myself is that a numbness of self-preservation limited my emotions at this young age. That I do not recall feeling any sense of panic while everyone was running around frantically shouting for my mother is a mystery to me. Do six-year-olds have a natural built-in obliviousness toward traumatic experiences? Surely this was one, especially since my mother soon followed my brother to the hospital, leaving me "alone" in the camp with only the other women prisoners and Auntie Vena to protect me.

Mother: *"Unbeknownst to me, Donald was sent off to a hospital to have his forehead stitched up and everybody came running over to tell me that he had gone. The panic I felt at the realization that Donald was no longer in the camp with me sent me flying out to the front of the building where we were forbidden to go, where I bumped into a Japanese officer coming in to inspect our camp. I was so agitated I grabbed him by his lapels and just about shook him silly, demanding to know what on earth he'd done with my son. I think he was so astonished that he actually offered to take me to see Donald in the hospital. He took me in his car, incidentally charging me ten guilders for doing it, but I saw Donald. He was unconscious in the hospital for about five days. I visited him daily, an ambulance taking me there and back, for which I had to pay each time. When Donald did regain consciousness, I insisted on bringing him back to the camp with me, although the doctor wanted to keep him in the hospital. But I said if anytime they moved me from that camp to another camp I wanted to have my son with me and not in a hospital where I couldn't get hold of him. Donald still has that scar as a reminder of that incident, although he cannot remember it."*

After the accident, Auntie Vena and my mother took turns telling us stories, and attempts were made to teach me to read. Usually a stick in the dirt had to make do for learning the alphabet and writing simple words. The fact that I eventually studied for a degree in geography at London University is a positive outcome of my mother's attempts to educate me in the concentration camps.

Auntie Vena also gave Ron, Donald, and me nature talks, pointing out flowers that blossomed within the campgrounds: morning glory, hibiscus, oleander. Large shrubs of hibiscus in the corner of the grounds provided hiding places for hide-and-seek or a quiet place to just sit with another child and tell stories to each other. The cooking area was fun to visit, although we were always shooed away by one of the women trying to concoct a meal for the group. Large iron pots on a black stove burbled away with rice or some kind of stew. As the weeks, passed the amount of food grew less and less.

Then something happened to Mother. Mother: *"About eight months after we'd been in the camp, I got blood poisoning in my right arm and I was ill with a very high fever. I was put in the little lean-to makeshift hospital. A very nice Jewish lady who was interned with us kept making me potions and giving them to me to drink and putting them on my arm like a poultice. The potions tasted terrible, very bitter, but I tried to swallow them. Nothing seemed to work and I was getting worse and worse and feeling like death warmed over. Fortunately for me, there was a cholera scare in the town and the Japanese doctor came to the camp to give everybody a cholera vaccination. That was the only time we ever saw a doctor come into the camp. He asked why I was in the lean-to. On diagnosing me, he gave me an injection for the blood poisoning (I didn't get the cholera shot). Whatever he injected me with did cure the blood poisoning and I fully recovered. For all the time we were in concentration camps, that was the only time I was very ill."*

My mother's illness and fever meant that she was not able to teach my brother and me or tell us stories. She could not participate in cleaning our space or do the duties around the camp required by our guards—no cleaning, no cooking like all the other women. It was a very anxious time for everyone concerned about her condition. I was allowed to visit her in the solitary "hospital" room, sitting by her on an upturned crate. I did this many times during the day to reassure myself that she was still there. It may have occurred to me that she might be whisked away suddenly, just as my brother had been after his accident. But fortunately she recovered quickly after getting her injection. We all got injections but she told me that hers was a different one to make her better. I presumably got the cholera injection, although I had no idea what that meant at the time, except that it hurt.

After we had been in the camp for ten months, we were moved to Tangatingey Concentration Camp. Once we were there, somewhat incredibly, Kleina Lengkong Camp began to seem like a rather nice interlude.

CHAPTER THREE

PRISONER

Tangatingey Camp
—A Real Prison

The truck bumped along the country roads for several hours, with a crowd of us packed into the back. It was hot and stuffy. Kleina Lengkong camp receded into the distance. Glimpses of villages, tropical foliage, banana plants growing along the roadside, and people wading in paddy fields flitted past us. Eventually, we were unloaded into a huge room in what was to become our second concentration camp—Tangatingey.

It was nighttime when we arrived. Yet again we were herded into strange surroundings, not knowing what was going to happen to us. When we were led into our quarters, I felt I was in a cage. Slatted bamboo platforms lined one side of the room, which was lit by one huge, very bright, bare overhead light bulb. Auntie Vena and Ron were with us, along with dozens of Asian women and children packed into the same room. Somehow we had gotten separated from the other British women—Aunty Vena, my mother, and we three children were the only Europeans in this room. The Asian women were dressed in their native dress called baju kebayas: batik sarongs, or long skirts with close-fitting tops called bajus. Most of these women had their black hair pulled back into a knot behind their head. They all spoke a different language from us. The commotion was incredible, what with the bright light, concrete floor, four walls closing us in, and the incessant chatter of women and children reverberating off the bare walls. I clung to my mother's side, feeling a security in her presence but also very bewildered and tired by the crush of people and the noise.

A Question of Nationality

Mother: *"When we got to Tangatingey, Vena and myself and you three children were a bit slow off the mark getting into the prison. Somehow we got separated from the British group from Kleina Lengkong and were put into a very large room with a number of Asian women. Now, these women were married to British subjects who had been living out in the Far East before the war and they were, all of them, dressed in sarongs and bajus. They had their children with them. There must have been fifty or even as many as eighty of them, I think, along with Vena and me, you, Donald, and Ron."*

"A Japanese officer eventually came into the room, a very short man with bandy legs and a very long sword that clanked behind him on the concrete floor. He took a look at all of the women in native dress with their children and then at the five of us and he shouted in broken English, 'All ingres that side, all no ingres this side,' pointing to opposite ends of the room. The Asian women and children moved over to the 'ingres' side and Vena and myself and you three children moved to the 'no ingres' side. He did a double take on that and decided we hadn't understood, so he repeated the order but in the opposite direction: 'All ingres over here, all no ingres over there.' So we all shifted places and he looked even more astonished. He came clanking up to us and pointed at Vena saying, 'You no ingres?' She said no, she was born in England

but had married a Dutch man and had taken Dutch nationality after she married. So therefore she was Dutch. He pointed to Ron and said, 'Where he born?' Vena said, 'In Borneo.' He stated, 'Oh, so he's Indonesian.' Vena exploded in his face with indignation and said her son wasn't anything of the kind; he was a perfect little Dutch boy. With each word she uttered she had moved closer up to the officer. The Japanese officer was very taken aback, his eyes almost popping out of his head at Vena's tirade.

"After she ran out of steam, he turned away from her and continued his questioning. Pointing to me, he said, 'What you?' I replied, 'I'm an American.' He then pointed to Phyllis: 'Where she born?' 'She was born in Mexico.' He pointed to Donald: 'Where he born?' 'He was born in Java.' Well, he decided, having had a mouthful from Vena, that he wasn't going to make any remarks about Donald's being Javanese. So he thought he'd get a jump ahead on that one and said, 'What's their father?' 'He's a Scotsman.'

"Without a word, the officer turned sharply away from us, but before giving the whole thing up, turned to the Asian women and asked them their nationality. 'English,' they all chorused in unison, 'we are married to Englishmen.' He paused barely a moment, turned on his heels, and clanked out of the room as his sword hit the ground with each step. That was the last we ever heard of the nationality problem."

Bedtime Prayers

Donald and I would sleep under the split bamboo slats, along with all the other children. It was the only way to avoid the brightness of the overhead light, which was left on all night. We were in this cage like room for many weeks. I recall very little of this episode except the feeling of being caged and confined, the bright light, and the cram of people in the same room.

Then, over the course of a few days, many other groups of European women and children arrived and were sorted out into various rooms and cells. Ultimately, there were about five hundred of us in this prison camp.

Mother: *"The Japanese in charge of this prison eventually arrived to sort us out. The prison was fan-shaped. It had five triangular wedge-shaped parts to it. Prisoners of war were put into two triangles, while the ordinary prisoners, the natives who were taken in for criminal offenses, were still in the other three parts of the prison. The entrance to each segment at the narrow end of the wedge also included an open space into which we were herded. This space lead to the outside main door and office of the prison warden. It was used as a craft room for the regular prisoners to make crafts for sale and to keep them gainfully occupied.*

"This camp was a real prison, a fairly new one, built by the Dutch before the war started. The Japanese authorities thought it would be best if they put all of the women and children in the two large rooms at one end of the triangles and all the single women in the cells of the two sections of the prison beyond the open rooms at the entrance. To house us in this fashion, they had made long benches of split bamboo for us to sleep on in the open sections at the entrance. Now, bamboo, when it is split lengthwise, is round on one side and hollow on the other, and they had laid it with the rounded part up. This gave us a corrugated washboard surface to sleep on. Another thing that split bamboo does

is breed bedbugs by the millions. So between the corrugated surface and the bedbugs, it was impossible to sleep. But the bamboo was the only thing in the room to sleep on. There was no other place except the ground itself. They also had a very large light in the room, which was left on all night. Its incredible brightness would have done fine service in a lighthouse. The adults found it impossible to sleep, from sheer discomfort. The children could fit underneath the split bamboo shelves, so they all slept there on the cement floor in the dark. Since the adults could not sleep, we took to playing bridge. I regularly played with three Malayan women. They were extremely good bridge players and played in the Malay language. I had some very good games with them.

"The noise that we generated when we were shut in at six in the evening until about eight the next morning when the doors were unlocked was absolutely unbelievable. The place was known as the 'fish market.' After about a month, the Japanese and the single women in the prison cells couldn't stand the noise. So they decided to reverse our arrangements and put all the single women in the fish market and put the mothers with children into the cells, one cell per family. We were put into a small cell. All it had was a drop-leaf shelf that could be pushed up during the day and let down for sleeping on at night. As the cells were overrun with rats, I put you two children on the drop-down bench to sleep, while I attempted to sleep on the floor between fighting off rats all night. So again I didn't get any sleep and instead did my sleeping in the daytime between the cleaning jobs the Japanese gave us. I was put on a duty in the prison camp with a famous concert pianist, Lili Kraus. Our job was to wash down the shower rooms and the toilets, which we did every day for the duration of the time we were in that camp."

After making the switch in accommodations, we were locked into a small prison cell every night as soon as the sun set and unlocked again every morning shortly after the sun rose. This was a frightening ritual. The guards made the rounds, shutting the cell doors with a resounding clang. After ours slammed shut, the sounds of the other cell doors banging and the sounds of the locks turning lasted some time before silence reigned in the prison.

It was about this time that I remember my mother teaching us to say our prayers every night. Once all the cell doors were shut, she sat us on the edge of the wooden board that served as a bunk bed and instructed us. I learned to say the Lord's Prayer: "Our father which art in Heaven, hallowed be thy name. Thy kingdom come, Thy will be done on earth as it is in heaven…" In addition, she had us recite the names of our relatives before going to sleep: "God bless Daddy, God bless Gran (my father's mother), God bless Auntie Joey (my father's sister), and Uncle Doug (her husband), and Isobel (my cousin), God bless Mummy, God bless Donald. My name is Phyllis Nisbet, my mother's name is Dorothy Nisbet, my father is Frank Nisbet, and his mother's name is Isabella Nisbet and she lives at Santa Aurora in North Berwick, Scotland." Every night as the prison door clanged shut, we recited this lineage and said our prayers. My small brother, who was now three years old, also had to learn this whole family recital: "My name is Donald Nisbet…." Once mother was satisfied that we knew the names of our family, we could go to sleep.

Donald and I slept with our heads at opposite ends of the bunk, with our bodies side by side, curled up against each other. I could feel his feet against my shoulder or arm as he slept on the inside next to the wall. We both fit on the shelf, while our mother sat on the floor. We simply went to bed with the clothes we had worn during the day, since we had no other clothes.

During the day, we ran around the compound inside the walls of the prison. At least it was clean, in contrast to all the other camps, as I recall them. Concrete surfaces made it easier to rinse and lots of water was available. Taps and hoses could be used to swoosh down the walls and floors. We even played in the spray of the hoses, enjoying the water and the coolness in the heat of the afternoon. Sprays of water catching the light of the sun sprinkled high into the air as we took turns to spritz the end of the hosepipe, pointing it skyward. It is a pleasurable memory of feeling clean and cool through laughter and play, a rare combination during those years.

NASI GOERING—A TREAT TO EAT

Mother: *"This was one of the cleanest camps of all the ones we were in. We could each of us get a shower every morning. Plus, Lili and I had the duty of cleaning the shower area every afternoon.*

"We'd been in the camp some weeks, when the regular prisoners in the other part of this prison establishment asked permission from the Japanese to send us some nasi goering. They were celebrating a special Malay feast day and had cooked up a mass of food for themselves. Feeling sorry for us women and children, they offered to share their food. Nasi goering is a fried rice dish, a specialty of Indonesia. As we were getting fewer and fewer rations week by week, this was naturally quite a treat for us. At the time that the fried rice was being distributed,

I was on cleaning duty with Lili, so Vena and you three children went off to collect our portion. When I eventually arrived back at the cell, Vena and you three had eaten your rice and mine was sitting in a coconut shell on the shelf, waiting for me. I sat down to eat it. You all sat in a circle and gazed at me with great big eyes while I ate my portion. This wasn't unusual because everybody was always so hungry that you looked with big eyes at anyone eating anything, anywhere. When I was all finished and had eaten the last grain of rice, you anxiously asked if I felt all right. And yes, I felt fine. Did I enjoy the rice? Yes, I enjoyed the rice very much. Well, said Vena, we didn't like to tell you until you ate it, but Donald was carrying your portion of rice and he dropped it in the ditch and we scraped it up and put it back in the bowl for you. I seemed to survive that, so it didn't matter too much. And the nasi goering was delicious.

"While we were in this prison camp, Ron became very ill with some mysterious disease. In fact, he was so ill with such a high temperature that he was taken into a room at the end of the fish market, which had been put aside for the sick. A number of Dutch women who belonged to the Salvation Army ran this hospital. Ron was presumably being looked after by these Dutch women until Vena checked up on him and found that he was getting thinner and hungrier and more lackadaisical every day. She discovered that none of the sick children in this so-called hospital were getting their food at all, that the women in charge were collecting the children's share of food and eating it themselves. Needless to say, Vena had Ron out of there in double-quick order. He finally did get better under Vena's care."

One of the lessons my mother regularly taught Donald and me was that there are good and bad people in every race and that we had to watch a person's behavior to tell the difference. Although I did not think it at the time, in retrospect, it is interesting to note the stark contrast between the generosity of the native prisoners who wanted to share their nasi goering with us, and the behavior of the Salvation Army hospital workers who ate the food of the sick children. That some people maintain their humanity even in the worst of circumstances, while others sink to the lowest level, says something about human nature. This truth may have seeped into my mind at a subconscious level, the two contrasting behaviors occurring in the same camp as they did.

Years later, my marriage to Torrey Pilgrim—I, a white woman married to a black man in 1950s England—brought me up against the prejudices of society. Even my parents were worried for me, but I always remembered the lesson of "good and bad in every race. " Torrey's and my interracial household was the hub of an international group, The Creative Association, the dream-child of my husband. Every Sunday evening for eight years, our home was open to as many as fifty people from a range of eighty countries, who passed through our door to discuss world issues and events. Later, when we moved to Barbados in 1968, Torrey's family embraced me lovingly, and I feel gratitude that I experienced a deep acceptance into a culture just emerging from its colonial ties into independence. Barbados gained its independence from Great Britain on November 30, 1966.

I have now traveled the world myself, and what I have learned in the context of "good and bad in all races" is that we are ultimately all human, wanting similar things for our lives: to love and be loved, to understand and be understood, to have friends and to make a living which hopefully honors our talents, to be part of a family, to have children, to have some clothing, a meal a day and a roof over our heads. No matter the circumstances of the wonderful people I have met, whether materially rich or poor, they all strive for the above in one way or another and they have all extended friendship to me, a stranger in their land.

SIMPLE SUMS

My reading lessons were put on hold in this camp because there were no sticks to write with or dirt to write on, but my mother told us stories whenever she had a spare moment from cleaning the showers or catching up on her sleep. These stories included many of the usual nursery tales and I especially remember "Jack and the Beanstalk," "Snow White and the Seven Dwarfs," and "Cinderella." She also attempted to give me some understanding of math—counting up to a hundred in English, reciting multiplication tables, and doing simple sums using her fingers and any objects lying around to teach me. Gradually, I came to understand the concept of addition and subtraction but at a very simple level, as she was not very good at it herself. Many years later, while studying in a grammar school in Essex, England, I was considered good at math and often came first in class. I remember thinking that despite the fact that I had had a very different beginning in my math education, I could still do well and thanked my mother for her attempts to teach me and give me an understanding of numbers.

No Hurry

After six months in the prison, we were shifted to a transit camp. We were told it was within walking distance. We walked through the countryside with its villages, tropical foliage, banana plants, and paddy fields. Distant mountains surrounded the valley we were walking through. People transplanting rice into the paddies stopped their work in the fields, standing knee deep in water to watch as we walked by. We Europeans must have been quite a sight to the locals as our entire prison camp walked past them along the country lanes to our next camp.

"Mummy, hurry, hurry," I begged my mother, to no avail. The long walk to the next camp seemed to take all day to me. I was not quite seven years old at this time, but remember running from the front of the line to the back. My friends and their mothers were at the front while my mother and Donald were at the back. I felt impatient with my mother; I kept urging her to speed up so that she, too, could be at the front with my friends and we could all be together. She calmly told me she had no intentions of hurrying, "Why should I hurry? I am enjoying being outside in the countryside, seeing people living their lives, admiring the plants and flowers and enjoying the scenery. Why should I hurry to be imprisoned? I am staying out for as long as possible. You go on and be with your friends, if you want. I'll stay back here with Donald and take my time." So that was how, after about two hours of walking, I arrived at the next camp first, a half-hour ahead of my mother and brother.

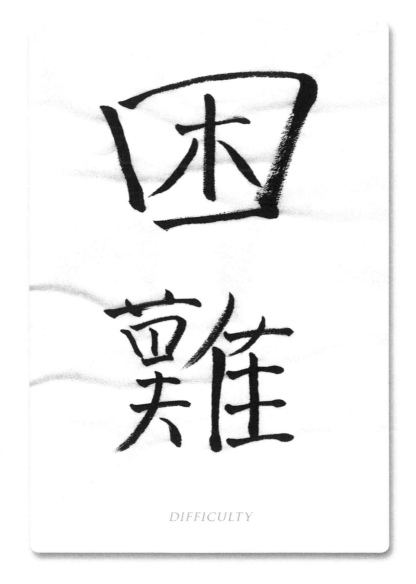

CHAPTER FOUR

DIFFICULTY

TANGARAY—A TRANSIT CAMP

When we got to the new camp, I was herded with my friends and their mothers into an enormous wire cage with a wooden wall at the back and was locked in. I was petrified, separated from my mother, and I screamed the place down. It seemed like forever before she arrived, when she was locked into a cage opposite me, way across the large compound. Confined separately, I remember thinking we would never be together again. A deep fear and panic gripped my whole body as I cried and shrieked for her. I heard her voice attempting to calm me down. But I was inconsolable and could only express my horror of being forever separated from her by wire walls. "It's all right, Phyllis, they will let us out soon," she called out to me. "They have to count us first; calm down."

The women around me did their best to calm me, too. I believe I did eventually, stuffing my fears deep inside, hanging onto the wire mesh, keeping my mother in sight across the way for fear she might disappear.

The counting took hours, but the Japanese were finally satisfied with their head count and opened the cages, allowing me to be reunited with my mother and brother. I clung to her side for many days while I recovered from my terror, if recovered is the word. My deep fright of finding myself separated from my mother in the third camp caused me to be very careful with whom I aligned myself in future years and to suffer considerable discomfort, even emotional trauma, when exposed to people who were chauvinistic, autocratic, or bullying. Eventually, I would learn to stand up for myself, but it was a long process that I did not fully comprehend. "Post-traumatic stress disorder" emerged as a field of study only since Vietnam. It was not a recognized condition when we returned to Britain after the Second World War. There, it was a matter of, "keep a stiff upper lip and get on with life." The British, after all, were recovering from their own traumas from their war with Germany.

THE KOREAN CAMP COMMANDANT

Mother: *"The Japanese had formed this POW camp out of one of their horse training camps. They converted it to gather together all the people from very small camps all over the island. Here they were going to reshuffle us, divide us up again, and redistribute us to larger camps. At Kleina Lengkong, there were about eighty of us. In the prison camp, we numbered about five hundred. And now in this transit camp we were about five thousand. This was the one and only time we were men and women together with children. Sadly, Daddy was not one of the men, and none of the men seemed to know of him or whether he was alive.*

"We were in the transit camp for about ten months. Since it had been a cavalry training school, its layout consisted of a very large U-shaped building, which comprised the stables before the war. Inside the U was an enormous cement space that had been used as a parade ground and behind that were fields where the horses had grazed during the day, although there were no horses while we were there. Again,

the Japanese had put up these split bamboo shelves for beds and in the stables there were three tiers of shelving, because the stables were much higher rooms than in the prison camp. As usual, I was the very last one to enter the place. For this reason we ended up on the top shelf of one of the stable rooms. Our sleeping space was in the far corner of the shelf and we had to climb up and down a ladder to get to our space. Fortunately, there was a window in our corner, which could open, providing us a view and some fresh air. Overlooking the front of the building, we could see down a very long road lined with palm trees on both sides. About a hundred yards beyond the walls of our building, a barbed-wire fence with guardhouses marked the outside boundary of our prison. Guards with bayonets and rifles stood on guard at the entrance to the prison.

"The man in charge of the transit camp was the only decent person we had in charge of us all the time we were in the camps. He came from South Korea. I don't quite know how he was put in charge of prisoners; I don't think he quite knew, himself. But he was an extremely nice person, felt very sorry for us, could do absolutely nothing to help us, but certainly did nothing to hinder us or harm us in any way. He had a most magnificent singing voice and could have done his country proud at the Metropolitan or anywhere else. He spent most of his evenings sitting out by the front of the building singing to himself and to the sky. As we slept overlooking the front door, we had a concert every night, which was lovely to listen to. On his small pay he bought fruit, which he used as prizes for games and races he organized for the children every week or so. He took a great interest in the children. He told us that he had two young children of his own and that he missed them *and all the children in the camp reminded him of them. He got the boys together and taught them judo, wrestling, and gymnastics. His weekly races were open to all the children. He would create all kinds of sports and competitions for them, resulting in each child getting a piece of fruit. You got a prize for coming in first, second, third… or last! He divided the fruit so that each child got a piece. He did this on a regular basis as long as he could afford it."*

BLACK PAPAYA SEEDS

We loved those days when we could compete in various races and get a piece of fruit. Donald always won a piece of fruit—a banana or a piece of papaya. He ran his heart out, determined to win and bring back his trophy—food. He always hoped for a piece of banana, which he usually got, not realizing that all the children "won" a piece of fruit no matter what place they came in the race. I loved papaya and would always hope for a piece of that fruit for my prize. Even today, the taste of the papaya I enjoy every morning at Rancho la Puerta puts me right back into our third camp, winning a sweet prize from the Korean captain. I often reflect on how interesting it is that a memory like that can stay with you for so many years, albeit a pleasant one within unfortunate circumstances.

My mother tried to get me to eat the black papaya seeds, saying they were very nutritious and good for me, but they were much too bitter and disgusting for my taste and I refused. She was loath to waste anything that was remotely edible and nutritious and to give her credit she did try her best to get me to eat them. Donald happily ate the papaya seeds for me. He loved their taste. The seeds are known to be anti-inflammatory and analgesic, which is possibly why my brother suffered very little from the many childhood diseases most other children suffered.

Aside from conducting athletic activities, the Korean guard was a gifted gymnast in his own right. He had a set of parallel bars and a high bar constructed in the yard, where he would practice daily. He swung his body round in huge circles and somersaulted off, landing with great agility. I was always very impressed and would watch him any time he practiced. He was always talking with us and telling us all kinds of stories about his family and his own children, as well as teaching us the skills of running, jumping, and gymnastics.

My mother continued to teach us as well as she could without the aid of books or writing tools. The stick drawn in the dirt continued to help me understand some words and recognize them when my mother wrote them out. It was tedious work. Her forte was in telling stories; painting word pictures as well as sketchy drawings in the dirt to further illustrate them. She was skilled at drawing comparisons with the things around us, regarding size, color, and shape. The size of a ship was compared to our living accommodations, the ocean compared to vast amounts of water as far as you could see, and the color of the water to the color of the sky. She was always trying to figure out ways to teach us. I know now that she must have been very concerned about our education or lack thereof and tried her best to make up for it.

Whenever the Korean commandant or some of the Japanese guards behaved kindly toward us prisoners of war, she would point out each kindness to Donald and me and say, "See, there is a good Japanese. He has helped that old woman up after she tripped over." Or, "The Korean commandant is a good person because he buys fruit for you as prizes for the races. Remember, there are good and bad individuals in every race, and when a person does nice things for others, then you know he is a good person." And, "See, Phyllis, that Japanese is a good person," pointing out yet another good deed, no matter how small, reinforcing the message that would resonate with me for the rest of my life.

"DON'T SCRATCH"

I must have passed my seventh birthday in this camp, but I cannot remember it at all. Perhaps it was during one of the times I was very sick. The first time I was ill, I had a very high fever and was covered with a rash all over my body. I remember the heat and feeling of weakness and lethargy. One of the ladies who claimed to know about such things said that my first illness was German measles, but no one really knew for sure. My mother kept me in the dark in the corner of the top shelf where we slept. She kept a cover over the window during the day so that the daylight would not affect my eyesight. She said the fever I had could damage my eyes if I was exposed to the bright sunshine of the tropics. I felt too ill to move, and the dimness of the daylight hours was deeply impressed on my mind. I stayed in the corner of the top shelf for many days. It may even have been several weeks. Going to the toilet was a big problem. I had to do it in an old tin can my mother found, and not spill any for fear of dripping it onto the shelves below. I was very careful, but it was difficult. Many of the women in the lower shelves complained bitterly about those children above them who did not control themselves. There were many arguments between women about their children. I did eventually recover and join the other children again.

My second illness was chicken pox. Scabs covered me from top to toe: back and front, arms, legs, face, and even my scalp. Gradually, these terrible scabs dried and itched like crazy. I was threatened within an inch of my life by my mother not to scratch or pick off any scabs. My mother covered my fingernails with cotton cloth to prevent my doing this, explaining that if I scratched off any scabs, I would be left with a scar indentation on that spot. If I did not want to be scarred for life, I must leave the scabs alone and let them fall off of their own accord. She impressed this upon me daily, at every opportunity that she came to see me or check up on me. I remember the discipline I felt within me, when I refrained from scratching although the urge was excruciating. What a temptation to do so, especially when the itching was terrible. I cannot imagine how I got through that ordeal but I did succeed, except for the last scab on my right temple, which I did scratch off. The light scar is there as a reminder to this day of my concentration camp chicken pox experience, and of the time I gave in to temptation. Donald did not get nearly as sick as I did on either occasion. He had a very light fever with the German measles and was up and about within a day or so, none the worse for it. And as for the chicken pox, he endured about five scabs in all. Maybe it was those papaya seeds he ate regularly, giving him the necessary protection from disease from those vitamins and minerals in the bitter black seeds.

"Sanitary" Arrangements

When I was not ill, I joined everyone else for the general toilet ar-rangements. This occurred outside the concrete compound, beyond the sheds where we slept. Here the camp opened out into a large field bounded by a deep roll of barbed wire fencing on two sides, sepa-rating us from the outside community. The very far end was actu-ally unfenced. A long trench was dug in this field. We literally had to straddle over this long, open ditch to go to the toilet in full view of everyone else. We all had dysentery or diarrhea and needed to go con-stantly. It was a common sight to see people running to this trench. I remember seeing old people trying to balance themselves over the ditch, not doing very well, and thinking how terrible that we could watch one another like this. This was my first real feeling of indignity and embarrassment at what should have been a private process. But I realized that everyone else was in the same situation. There was very little water—almost none to use, so we all got very dirty. This was undoubtedly the dirtiest of all the camps we were in.

On one occasion in the toilet area, I saw a woman shout out in indignation that someone had stolen her small piece of soap, which she had jealously guarded to wash her hands at the one and only wa-ter tap after using the toilet trench. She had placed the soap on the ground next to her foot, but someone had deftly taken it while she was busy straddling the trench and took her eye off the soap for an instant. She was heartbroken and frantic at her loss and wailed in indignation, cursing and imploring everyone around to give it back to her. But it was never found again and certainly no one admitted to taking it. Years later while I was recalling this incident with my mother, she, too, remembered it and told me that this was the only time she ever heard of anyone stealing anything from another person throughout the camp years.

Mother: *"The buildings had never been used as living quarters. There was only one tap that provided water and there were no sanitary arrangements at all except for the long ditch in the field at the back. It had no running water through it. Straddling it with a long line of men and women relieving themselves out in the open was a most disgusting experience, which none of us could avoid. As we were fed only on very rough corn for the first five days we were in the camp, everybody had diarrhea and everybody was squatting in rows behind each other over this ditch. The stench and the commotion were indescribable. There was no way to clean yourself, there was no way to wash, and there was no way to get yourself better.*

"The corn we were given to eat was chicken-feed corn, not sweet corn, and it was only occasionally served with a ration of rice. More often than not, the corn was riddled with weevils and tiny insects and we just had to eat what we were given. That was all we ate while we were in that camp—no meat and no vegetables. The Japanese said there was nothing else and even they had to eat it, so they were no better off than us. Sometimes the corn was cooked and sometimes it was raw—you just chewed on it. Because that was all we had to eat, we all continued to have the runs.

"This field was open at the far end to the outside world, but we were not allowed to wander too far in that direction. The Japanese guards saw to that. A very unusual group of people camped at the end of the

field, well beyond the toilet trench. I could see them—people with green hair. They were pale-skinned, not Asian. Men, women, and children all spoke a strange language, unlike any I had heard. I knew what Hungarian sounded like from hearing Lili Kraus speak, and it certainly wasn't that. Nor was it like any Asian language. No one else knew what to make of them, either. They did not seem to be guarded by the Korean or Japanese guards but lived their own lives at the end of the field, separate from the rest of us. I tried to approach them on several occasions, curious to know more about them, but they acted in a threatening way toward me when I got too close, so I backed off. I never did find out who they were or where they came from."

A Birthday Gift

Sometime during those months in that camp, I received a gift from my mother's friend Lili Kraus, probably for my seventh birthday. It was a beautifully embroidered handmade Hungarian doll. It was exquisite, and I loved and treasured it for many years. It had a delicate face drawn in pencil on pale pink cotton stockinet cloth. Its head and body was tightly stuffed, very firmly made and finely stitched. The doll's outfit included a lace petticoat with a wide black satin skirt over the top of it. The bottom edge on one side of the skirt was stitched up to the waist, with the doll's hand holding it in place. Her white bodice was delicately folded in little pleats, and her skirt embroidered with rows of delicate rosebuds in all shades of pink. A circular pillbox hat embroidered with colorful threads in vertical stripes around the edge of the hat completed the outfit. She was enchanting. How Lili got the materials for this doll under the conditions we were in, I cannot now imagine. But many of the women spent endless hours sewing with what they had, redesigning outfits as clothes wore out, cutting them down for children's clothes, then using whatever cloth as was left to make little gifts.

My mother had a small collection of needles in a little crocheted hat with layers of cloth underneath to hold the needles. The hat was in the shape of a wide-brimmed sombrero. Her thimble fit into the space for the head. One of the women in the camp had crocheted it as a gift for her, and she has it to this day. Threads were rescued by unraveling cloth, or carefully unpicking old seams, jealously guarded, and saved for future use.

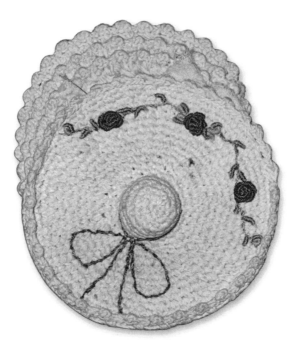

Crocheted sombrero-hat for holding needles and pins

Before the war started, my mother had had all my little dresses and bloomers made by a local Chinese tailor in Tjepoe; she had then added some embroidery, appliqués, or rickrack to most of my outfits. In the camp she managed to use what was available to continue these embellishing skills with whatever was available. Great ingenuity resulted in some very interesting creations. My mother continued to embroider well into her eighties, creating fine "paintings" in thread. This hobby was surely honed during these concentration camp years.

CHRISTMAS CONCERT

Mother: *"One of the very nicest things that ever happened to us happened in this transit camp during the Christmas of 1943. I think I mentioned before that I had as my cleaning mate in the previous camp a lady called Lili Kraus, who was a very famous international pianist. She had been separated from her husband and children when her ship was wrecked on the way to New Zealand. She was on her way from Europe to give a concert in New Zealand. She was picked up by the Japanese and put into our camps. She asked if it was possible to give a concert on Christmas Eve and the Korean captain with the lovely voice readily agreed.*

"There was a gentleman in the camp called Goldberg who was an international violinist. He had been allowed to keep his Stradivarius violin; the Japanese had not taken it away from him. Lili asked Goldberg to play with her in the concert. Another lady in the camp was a professional jazz pianist, so she was asked to perform a jazz piece for the concert. In addition, several young teenagers who had been taught ballet before the war put together an act. Gradually, an

entire Christmas concert was organized with children dancing, a choir singing, followed by the jazz pianist. Lili Kraus and Goldberg performed the grand finale.

"The Japanese said the concert could last for four hours. It was a beautiful moonlight night on Christmas Eve and, being in the tropics, of course, it was warm. We all sat on the cement in the parade ground; the Japanese sat on chairs in front of the piano. And after the lesser lights had done their turns, Lili and Goldberg came forth to do their concert. Lili played solo piano, specializing in Chopin. Then she and Goldberg together played every classical concert piece they could remember. Each then played violin and piano solos. The concert was supposed to last from eight p.m. until midnight, but we were still sitting there when the sun came up. It was a beautiful night, balmy and warm with a full moon. The Japanese allowed the concert to go on and on and on, as enthralled by it all as we were. The players never even stopped for breath. What could be more beautiful than this gem of talent in the midst of war and squalor? It was a treat, never to be forgotten. It was, and still is, the most beautiful concert I have ever heard. It was absolute pure heaven that night.

"After the war, I met up with Lili again. When she came to London for a concert, I got in touch with her. She said that she and Goldberg had gone to a studio, paid for it, and arranged to record every tune they had played that night at the Christmas concert in the camp. I asked if it was possible to get hold of a copy, I would have loved to have a copy of it, but she said, 'I'm sorry, no. We just made it for the two of us. I did have an extra copy made for Mrs. Olsen, the governor's wife, but that was all, there are no extra ones.

"One of the Japanese officers present at the concert was a very good amateur pianist and asked Lili if she would give him piano lessons. He said that if she would do so, he would arrange for her to be taken to the camp where her husband was. He would also try to find her children and bring the four of them together in exchange for her giving him lessons for the duration of the war. She did do this, and was reunited with her family in another camp. At the end of the war, she told me that she had continued on to New Zealand with her family and completed the concert tour, which she should have done three and a half years earlier.

"Just as a footnote, I might say that the Japanese always sang when they lowered their flag down the mast every evening. Their voices were very beautiful, reminding me very much of the Welsh male voices. For some unknown reason they sang words in Japanese, but always to the tune of 'Loch Lomond.' It always sounded so incongruous, but very lovely, nevertheless."

FOOD PARCELS

Food parcels! The arrival of truckloads of American Red Cross packages transported into our camp one day caused great excitement. In our semi starved state, the thought of extra food, no matter what it was, created an uproar. How was it to be distributed to all the prisoners of war? There were at least five thousand of us in this camp. There was great excitement as the contents of the boxes were gradually revealed. It was the luck of the draw as each prisoner of war lined up to get his or her one can of food from the packages. For some reason my mother, being an American, was given a whole box to herself.

It was filled with canned goods: milk, sardines, salmon, corned beef, plus packets of crackers. It was amazing. Certainly we shared our bonanza with Auntie Vena and Ron and a few of our friends.

One of the women my mother had played bridge with in the second camp in the fish house, a Malayan woman with two small children, longed for a can of salmon, but did not get one in the distribution. We knew her very well, and I played with her children. My mother, seeing her bitter disappointment, gave her one of the five cans of salmon from our parcel. I will always remember her radiant, joyful expression, as she was given this treasure. She could not thank my mother enough, wringing her hands in gratitude as tears streamed down her face. Our cans of salmon were in great demand. Auntie Vena and Ron got one, a neighboring family another, and we ate the remaining two ourselves. The taste of canned salmon, the soft bones, its juiciness, its delicious flavor was indescribable, and I measured everything thereafter by the standard of canned salmon. It was the most wonderful food I had ever eaten.

One other food stands out from this time. Our Malay friend occasionally created delicious rice treats by holding back some of her ration when we were given boiled rice, which was not often. She mixed the cooked rice with a small combination of oils and sugar, which she obtained from some mysterious source. She had found a metal tray somewhere and spread the rice mixture thinly over it to dry in the sun, which produced this magical delight: crunchy texture and sweet taste in the midst of hunger and famine. I loved to watch her make it and she happily shared some of it with Ron, Donald, and me, along with her own children.

Shortly after the excitement of the food parcels, we were to be moved again. We had been in this camp for about ten months.

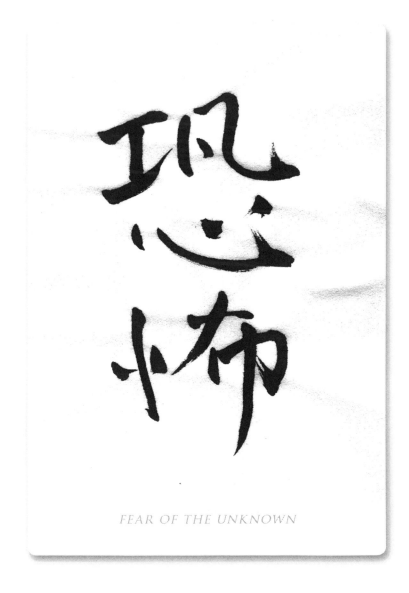

CHAPTER FIVE

FEAR OF THE UNKNOWN

A Train Journey

The Japanese rallied us all into the middle of the parade ground, sorting us into groups, calling names, and shunting us from one section of the parade ground to another, arranging us in long lines. It became clear that my mother, Donald, and I were to leave the camp. Auntie Vena and Ron were to stay behind. We sadly said good-bye to them with hugs and kisses, wondering if we would ever see them again.

Out in the hot sun, we waited our turn to be led from our bleak but familiar world. Our Malay friend ran up to us and pressed a small package of sandwiches into my mother's hand as a parting gift. Since we were given no food or water to take with us, this was an act of enormous generosity and a wonderful gift by way of a thank-you for the can of salmon. The sandwiches were filled with cabe (pronounced chabay), a spicy paste made from hot pepper. It was all she could find to give to us, but the unexpected gesture of gratitude and friendship made an impression on me. To be given food by a fellow prisoner was a no small act. The smell was delicious, and made my mouth water. My mother kept the sandwiches safely in her one bag, to be eaten later.

I often wonder about our Malay friend and her kindness to us. Her generous gift under those circumstances is never to be forgotten, as undoubtedly was our gift of salmon to her. Cabe sandwiches and salmon are two of my outstanding memories of food from those years, as are the crispy rice delicacies prepared by the Malay women in our camp. These outstanding tastes offered now and then as gifts are the food experiences I remember vividly from that time. The food provided by the Japanese on a daily basis was so meager and lacking in taste that I have little recollection of it. Mostly I recall the feeling of being perpetually hungry.

We were marched to the train, a long line of cars on a railway siding. We were literally herded into these cattle cars, which had iron sides, large sliding metal doors, and no windows. We were packed into an already packed car. My mother, always managing to be last in line, kept us close to her. Being the last on board the train, we ended up against the sliding door. There were narrow slatted cracks in the door, so we could see out just a little through the slats—and these gave us some fresh air. We were tired, hot, and dirty. No one had food or water. All we had was our small package of cabe sandwiches. Everyone who was packed into the train had to stand upright for the whole journey since there was no room to sit or lie down. The train did not go very fast, and stopped for long periods of time. By day we could see glimpses of the countryside through the cracks in the door.

Going to the toilet was an appalling business, trying to use one corner of the car only. It was a mess and the car stank of sewage, dirty bodies, and death. The journey seemed to last for a long time; day and night came and went more than once. The stench of toilet and sickness reeked in the heat. Several people collapsed next to us during the course of that journey. Some died, crumpled to the floor of the train. I asked my mother why people were collapsing and not moving. "What has happened to those people?" I asked.

"They are too tired to stand. Several people have died because of the lack of air and food," was her straightforward explanation. "And what is death?" I asked. "Sleeping forever," my mother said to her seven-year-old daughter.

I turned my eyes away from my first view of death, preferring to look out of the slats of the door to the glimpses of trees outside. The alarmed, crammed feeling I felt was probably claustrophobia, although I could not put a word to it at that age.

Later, as a teenager growing up in Scotland and England, I was always nervous about being in crowds or in confined spaces and avoided them as much as possible. My father once took me to a football match in Wembley Stadium in London to watch his beloved Arsenal team play. The stadium was packed and we sat high up in one corner surrounded by howling fans: forty thousand people attended that match and I was horrified to be packed in the midst of them. When the game ended I refused to move until most of the spectators had left. I did the same when I attended matches as an adult. Ultimately I would overcome my claustrophobia in Barbados, when I took my students to explore the island's underground limestone caves and breathed through the panic to gaze with awe and wonder at the beauty of the stalactites and stalagmites. But on this day, on that awful train, there was nothing to do but turn my head as one day blurred into another in this endless nightmare. When was it going to end?

Mother: *"Yes, we were the last to arrive at the train. I dawdled again and was at the end of the line, but this time I hung on to the two of you and didn't let you run back and forth. We walked to the train, and were the very last to get in—but being last, we at least had* air. While we were on the train, I lost track of time. I couldn't tell you exactly how long we were in there. We had these little sandwiches. I parceled them out among the three of us. We didn't eat them all at once. It was a blessing to be near the doors. The cold night wind coming in through the slats, especially while we were up in the mountains, gave us some respite. So that's again where we came out lucky with my dawdling.

"We were at least forty-eight hours in the train, or perhaps even two and a half days. We were shunted into sidings and left at a standstill for hours. It wasn't all that far from Bandung down to Batavia, but our captors took their time getting us there. That train trip was probably one of the worst experiences of my life. There was nothing I could do to protect my children from this horrifying experience. What explanation could I give? I felt heartsick and tried to think of happier times, but the horror, hunger, and human suffering we experienced was overwhelming."

I don't actually remember getting off the train. Many of those hours toward the end of the journey blurred together into one long, anesthetized terror. Filth, foul smells, and my first close encounter with the dying, linger as vague impressions. How we got from the train to our next camp is a complete blank in my mind.

CHAPTER SIX

DANGER & OPPORTUNITY

Tjideng Camp:
Prisoners in the Suburbs

Arriving at Tjideng, it was clear we were entering part of a city with regular houses and gardens. We were allocated to a real house. High rolls of barbed wire or regular barbed-wire fences marked the boundaries of the camp. The activities of the town and country folk beyond could be seen through the coils of wire. The dense rolls of wire were only about six feet wide between us and the outside world, so we could see through to where local people were going about their business close by. Some of the coils were nailed to tall posts embedded in the ground.

The first house we lived in was on one of the side street. It seemed very spacious to me after the overcrowding of our previous camps and the horrors of the recent train ride. We shared a room with an elderly Dutch lady called Mrs. Nordhoekhecht. She slept in a real bed surrounded by a mosquito net. We slept on the floor in the same room. It was a major improvement to live in a room in a real house with only four of us in the one room. That soon changed as more people were brought into the camp. Our house gradually filled up to a total of about forty people over the next few days. But at first it felt very pleasant and the room seemed cool and shady with trees near the house. We would be here for several months before moving to another house.

Mother: *"Tjideng camp was actually carved out of a part of the city of Jakarta (previously known as Batavia under Dutch rule). It consisted of a number of small houses, like a suburb with neighborhood streets. It had been fenced in with barbed wire to use as a POW camp. Within a few months of our arrival, there were about fifteen thousand women and children in the camp, as more and more women and children were packed into the tiny houses in Tjideng. We spent over eighteen months at this camp—until the end of the war, when only about half that number was still alive.*

"We shared our first house with an elderly lady, Mrs. Nordhoekhecht, who had been with us right from the early days in Kleina Lengkong. She was a Dutch woman in her seventies, quite tall and upright in stature, with a full head of very white hair. She was a handsome woman, distinguished looking and very charming. Her son was in the American navy and, unfortunately, was killed when the ships were bombed in Pearl Harbor."

MEETING CAPTAIN SONEI

"Bow and what you think is your own business." These words ring in my ears from Tjideng Camp. My mother's determination that both Donald and I obey the order to bow every time we passed a Japanese soldier on the road was drilled into our brains with daily reminders.

She impressed upon us the vital importance of bowing. "If you don't bow, I get punished," she said. She taught us to bow from the waist with our arms at our sides, looking at the ground. "If you look up while you bow, it will be regarded as an insult to the emperor of Japan, so make sure you bow properly." I have no idea what I thought at the time, but I did as I was told. The act of bowing in the proper manner was crucial to our collective safety. I understood that. The mothers of children who did not bow or forgot to bow were severely punished. I saw women with shaved heads walking around the camp. "Why are their heads bald?" I asked my mother. "Because they disobeyed the Japanese one way or another; probably didn't bow properly. If a Japanese soldier doesn't think you've bowed properly, you are punished. Shaving off a woman's hair is one form of punishment," she replied.

Other punishments included lessened food rations, hard labor and, occasionally, beatings. Witnessing these punishments meted out to some of the women in neighboring houses was traumatic for everyone. Seeing women having their heads shaved—often screaming at the indignation of the treatment, and then being slapped into submission for the deed to be done—and then watching those women walk around the camp without their hair made a big impression on me. I considered it a frightful situation. I was going to bow no matter what my thoughts were or were not supposed to be.

Later, this deeply embedded obedience response played out in my teenage years. I bowed to the wishes of my teachers, who were kind enough but strict and brooking no nonsense in postwar England. I was able to join the school system after a year of at-home tutoring to catch me up, but the regimentation—gated playgrounds, lining up for assembly, bells ringing—was stressful. And who knew what would happen if you didn't comply? Eventually, I suppose I was able to sort out the difference between blind obedience and discipline, and no doubt did quite well, becoming "head girl" of my grammar school:

a leader in my own right. On reflection, I doubt I did much in the way of leadership, though; rather, I worked out and did what was required of me in that position—still bowing, as it were, to the expectations of others.

Mother: *"The Japanese officer in charge of Tjideng camp was a man called Captain Sonei. Standing about five feet seven inches tall, he nevertheless had a very commanding presence. His posture was erect and he had a piercing gaze. Whenever he walked around the camp, it was with a crisp stride, taking everything in as he went. The guards under his command saluted him when he passed. We had to bow. Sonei was always immaculately dressed in his uniform, although he had this strange habit of wearing bedroom slippers for most of the month, except during the few days around the full moon. Then he wore his heavy, military boots with metal pointed tips.*

"Now, I had read in the past that there were people who went mad with the full moon—literally lunatics. I've only ever met one in my whole life and that was Captain Sonei. And what he could think up come full moon was unbelievable and indescribable. I cannot speak, to this day, of some of the atrocities he performed. They were that inhuman. Even thinking about them makes me feel sick to my stomach. I cannot sit near a Japanese person today without those feelings of revulsion welling up in me, although I realize they must be perfectly decent people. The association is too great for me to forget. I experience this physical revulsion welling up in my body, which reminds me of those atrocities, even though intellectually I know that I am in a safe place today."

Before every full moon anxiety spread through the camp as women wondered what Sonei would do this time. During one full moon,

Sonei was on the rampage again. "Look out, he has his metal-tipped boots on. He'll think up something vicious," I heard the women in our house saying. With his bedroom slippers gone, Sonei reduced everyone to a state of terror. The news spread through the camp, creating an underlying murmur and low conversations between the women in the various houses. I heard my mother and Mrs. Nordhoekhecht scheming up a plan to work around the horror they'd heard would be enacted that evening. It was something my mother did not want Donald or me to see.

The entire camp was to be counted again, another tenko, the tallying of all the prisoners. The Japanese regularly counted us. We stood in rows out in the main street for hours on end, but usually during the day. This time it was to be to be done in the evening.

Bowing

"You and Donald must stay in the house with Mrs. Nordhoekhecht. I don't want the two of you to see what the Japanese will do tonight. You must both hide under the bed, hidden by the mosquito net. When the guards come around they won't see you," Mother assured us. "Don't make a noise," she warned as she went off with the other women.

Donald and I huddled under the bed, peering through the net toward the door, with Mrs. Nordhoekhecht sitting bolt upright in a chair, facing the door. With her back to us, she proceeded to ruffle up her very white hair so that it stood out dramatically from her head. From our viewpoint under the bed it looked as if there was a large white cloud around her head, which would later shine brilliantly in the moonlight. Nothing happened for several hours. Then footsteps in the distance and banging doors alerted us to the routine inspection of houses by Japanese soldiers. They were coming closer. Mrs. Nordhoekhecht turned and put her fingers to her lips to indicate to us to be silent.

Donald and I threw our arms around each other and held tight as we watched the guard enter our house. The instant he entered, Mrs. Nordhoekhecht leapt out of her chair, screeching ferociously and waving her arms frantically as if to attack the guard. The sound from her throat was terrifying, a ghostly, guttural sound giving the impression she was completely mad. Donald and I hugged each other tighter. The petrified Japanese soldier turned on his heels and ran out of the house, not to be seen again that evening. Mrs. Nordhoekhecht returned to her chair and leaned back quietly and told us to stay under the bed just in case he did return. We fell asleep there with her sitting upright all night, facing the door. My mother returned with the other women in the early morning hours. Although my mother refused to speak of it to Donald or me at that time, we knew something terrible had happened because everyone was in such a state of tears, horror, and exhaustion, but I never learned the details until many years later.

Mother: *"It was a nauseating experience. During that full moon, Sonei ordered all the dogs in the camp to be killed. I heard about what was going to happen ahead of time and didn't want you and Donald to see anything so cruel. So I hid you under Mrs. Nordhoekhecht's bed and suggested she stay in the house and act mad if any Japanese came along. For some reason, best known to themselves, the Japanese revere elderly people and fear madness. Mrs. Nordhoekhecht readily agreed to the scheme. Instead of tenko, we were forced to watch these poor animals being beaten to death. The Japanese guards tied all the dogs up into sacks and forced the young boys—those under eleven who were staying with their mothers—to beat them with sticks until they were dead. Not one dog was allowed to remain alive. Most of the dogs had become pets for the children. The boys were in tears and totally distraught as they were forced to beat the sacks with the dogs yelping inside. The anguished sounds of dogs yelping and boys sobbing filled the night air. The mothers of the boys and all the other women forced to look on helplessly were filled with anguish and despair to see such a thing happen to these children and their pets. The physical and psychological cruelty was almost unbearable. The ordeal took all night. The whole scene was sickening and seemed interminable. Of course, I kept wondering the whole time during this nightmare whether I had done the right thing by leaving you two children behind. What if the guards found you? I was sick inside with worry. Mrs. Nordhoekhecht later told me your experience. She reckoned that she'd done the best acting job of her life. Fortunately for us, all the guards didn't search far enough to find you two children underneath her bed. I found you still there fast asleep the next morning."*

TENKO: THE COUNTING DAYS

Tenko was a regular occurrence and the bane of every prisoner's life. The entire camp of fifteen thousand women and children lined up in the streets in rows to be counted by the Japanese, who counted out loud in their own tongue: Ichi, ni, san... (one, two, three...). Sonei marched up and down along the front of the rows, checking the accuracy of the numbers. We often stood for hours in the hot sun while the tabulation of the many thousands of prisoners took place to his satisfaction. It seemed as if he was never satisfied. Our lines often got counted over and over again. Many arguments broke out between the women at the head of each line and the soldier responsible for counting the row with her. Such arguments between a soldier and a woman brought Sonei to the scene, demanding an explanation from the woman "in charge" of her line. A stumbling explanation or a cowed expression usually resulted in a cruel beating from Sonei's whip, a thin lath-like stick, which swished wickedly through the air. Many a tenko resulted in screams, cuts, bruises, and women being beaten to the ground.

During the full moon phase, Sonei's big iron-tipped boots shone in the moonlight or glittered in the noonday sun. He had everyone trembling at the sight, not knowing what he might do next. Witnessing a frail woman being kicked viciously during one tenko, I asked my mother why she was being kicked. She hushed me quickly, putting her hand over my mouth. Later, she explained that Sonei went mad during the full moon. "He is a lunatic in the true sense of the word. There is no knowing why he does anything during these times." That was the first time I learned the meaning of lunatic. It was something fearful, indeed. Everyone was overwhelmed with a sense of repression and intense caution at these times, for fear of terrible reprisals. Everyone kept as quiet and still as possible so as not to draw attention to themselves during the tenko hours.

On one occasion when Sonei was on the rampage, questioning the accuracy of the numbers of people in each line, the woman at the head of the line next to ours was whipped for her apparent inaccuracy. At our line, the number was again in doubt, with a discrepancy between my mother's count and the soldier's. The moment Sonei raised his whip to strike my mother, she as quickly jabbed her left index finger to her right upper arm, turning her arm to face him. She was pointing to the American flag embroidered on her armband, looking with defiance straight at Sonei. (We were all required to wear armbands with our national flag.) He lowered his whip and moved on. Our whole line sighed with relief and astonishment at my mother's bold act.

"If you stand up to Sonei, he seems to let you alone," was my mother's opinion. She often imparted this advice to the other women.

Looking back, I am in awe that my mother was able to stand up to Captain Sonei. In my teenage years, after the war, I considered my mother's "dominating" personality off-putting, and tried to distance myself from her whenever possible. But I see now that her dominating streak—perhaps better described as strength of character undoubtedly helped her survive many of Sonei's tirades and cruelties.

Mother: "One peculiar aspect of tenko, and the source of many problems in getting an accurate count for each line, was the fact that most of the Japanese guards could not count past ten. Yet Sonei insisted that the lines have fifteen persons in each line. I quickly figured out a way, with the guard counting with me, to use the fingers of both hands to establish the number fifteen in our row: ten fingers for both hands followed by five fingers of one hand usually got the job done without a problem. It was only on that one occasion, that a new guard allocated to my line would not accept the repeated hands and fingers solution but insisted on counting once through only. He just could not count past ten in Japanese! It was amazing and most frustrating. All the women knew how to count to fifteen in Japanese that was for sure. When a guard misnamed the subsequent numbers after ten, arguments inevitably arose. I was fortunate not to get beaten. The American flag seemed to command some respect from Sonei—either the flag or my quick response and defiant attitude, or perhaps both, saved me from a beating."

I remember many a tenko out in the blazing sun. Even though my sense of time for that period of my life is vague today, one tenko may have taken as long as three days, without food or water. Days and nights went by, hot during the days out in the open sun, cooler during the nights with the full moon. We were required to stand the whole time, which made it very trying for young children and old people. Each line tried to take it in turns for one or two of us to rest on the ground at the back, while those in front were on the lookout for the guards when they approached. When that happened, word got to the back of the line for anyone lying down to stand up immediately with minimum fuss, and for young children to be held. I remember being wakened from sleeping on the ground at the end of our line and made to stand up quickly, in time for Sonei to walk by without noticing. Our line seemed to manage this ordeal fairly well without getting caught. The exhaustion, heat, fear, and survival tactics of those days of tenko are indelibly ingrained in my mind.

One of the horrifying memories of tenko my brother reminded me about was the time Sonei was in a frenzy over the supposed "disobedience" of a woman lying exhausted on the ground in the line next to ours, during a particularly long counting session. No amount of shouting or kicking could get the woman to her feet. Sonei finally unsheathed his sword intending to kill the woman, when the soldiers with him restrained him, pulling him back strongly, speaking in rapid-fire Japanese and presumably urging him not to strike. Sonei yielded. He collected himself, strode past several lines, and beheaded an Asian woman standing at the head of her line. Everyone froze with shock instantaneously. This was undoubtedly Sonei's "saving face" and establishing his authority in front of everyone. He coolly strode on with his inspection of the lines, leaving the dead woman on the ground. I was eight years old when this occurred, my brother five.

Many years later, I learned that the British captured Sonei at the end of the war. His captors, not entirely convinced of his atrocities, sought to question women who had been in Tjideng. The women were so distraught at the sight of Sonei that they reportedly almost lynched him. Their testimony left no doubt as to his cruelty and guilt. But Sonei proclaimed his innocence to the end, confessing only to giving some prisoners "a light slap on the face" and "pricking one woman on the leg with a stick" for using the term "Jap." He was charged with organized violence and cruelty toward civilians, and was executed in September 1946. On the day of his execution, Sonei asked in which direction Japan lay, turned toward his homeland, raised both hands in a two-handed salute and shouted, "Banzai, banzai, banzai" in the Bushido tradition of samurai warriors. Then he faced a firing squad of seven Dutch soldiers.

Although I did not learn of Sonei's fate for quite some time, he and his men had a powerful impact on my own fate for many years, in terms of my relationship to men. Many women who have not literally been prisoners of men nonetheless suffer from the effects of male dominance, but my years spent under the subjugation of Japanese men—cruel commandants and soldiers in four different camps—certainly did not provide me with good examples for male behavior.

Back in Europe after the war, I was fortunate to have a loving and understanding father and uncle to help counteract the images of Sonei and his minions. Yet, in the company of authoritarian men, I would clamp down emotionally. An emotional constriction of sorts and a stunted ability to communicate would creep over me. This gave me the appearance of shyness, withdrawal, and—as my first husband later described it (to my horror)—"emotional stultification."

When I first attended a coed school in Scotland after my private tutoring was completed, boys and girls often surrounded me in the playground asking me what it was like to be in a Japanese concentration camp. I felt terrified when an older, larger boy came right up to me demanding a response, poking me in the shoulder. I was speechless, and I physically curled up by bringing my arms across my body and lifting my knee up to protect myself. Unfortunately, the knee caught the boy in his groin and he backed off in pain. I was then in deep trouble for "attacking" the boy but was unable to explain my behavior to the head principal. I had no skills to confront questioning in the face of authority.

I quickly learned to stay away from certain kinds of people as much as possible, to avoid such confrontations, and did not make too many friends. Even when there were no men around, I steered clear of any situation with a hierarchy. I adamantly refused to join the Brownies, a younger version of the Girl Guides organization, since doing so required wearing brown uniforms, embracing all sorts of rules and regulations, and having to stand in military-like rows during roll calls—a frightening reminder of tenko.

A SHAVED HEAD

I celebrated my eighth birthday in Tjideng. My mother often brushed my auburn hair and twisted it into long ringlets down to my shoulders. A great storyteller, she accompanied the hair brushing with stories of the many countries she had lived in around the world. It was during these hair-brushing sessions that she noticed sores forming on my scalp, which were getting progressively worse. "You'll have to have your hair cut off if you want your scalp to get better," my mother declared. I was devastated... and this just before my eighth birthday. The only remedy my mother could think of was to shave my head and let the fresh air and sun heal my scalp. My thick hair and lovely long auburn ringlets were a hindrance and had to come off, to allow the sunshine to rid my scalp of disease. The association with those women who had their hair cut off as punishment was worse to me than the scalp disease: Would everyone think that I had not bowed properly? Would other children jeer at me, as I had seen some of the older boys do to the women who had their heads shaved? I begged and begged not to have my hair cut. But my mother was adamant. She had saved some precious medicine from the Red Cross package, which could heal my scalp more efficiently if I had no hair.

"Could we wait until after my birthday?" I asked. "Yes, that would be fine." To make it up to me, a very nice birthday was celebrated with gifts made from what was available. A new yellow dress with pretty blue buttons was the best gift, with several embroidered knickknacks added for good measure. I was very happy with the dress, and especially with the little blue buttons down the front, but not so happy with the prospect of having my head shaved the next day.

Off came the hair. I imagined the worst and insisted on wearing a bandana, a white triangular cloth wrapped completely around my head, tied in a knot on my forehead. I was determined to hide my baldness. It was almost a full year, just before my ninth birthday, before I was conscious of having a full head of hair again. My mother tried many times during the year to assure me that my hair had grown long again, that it looked very nice, that no one would know it had been shaved, but I did not believe her and wore the bandana despite her assurances. Only when I felt long curls down my neck again did I abandon that bandana.

Clothing was always a problem. We got progressively more and more ragged. But coming to Tjideng gave us more resources. We used curtains, sheets, and cushion covers from the abandoned Dutch homes we were crowded into to make new clothes. The yellow cloth of my dress had been a curtain! It was my first new dress since the start of the war years in the camps.

Mother: *"My clothing at this time was verging on the indecent. Rags hung all around my shoulders and hips, barely covering me. Arriving in Tjideng, I found two reasonably new red-and-white checkered tea cloths in our house and made them into the briefest of bikinis to cover me. The cloth was a thick, sturdy waffle weave, typical tea towel material, and this outfit lasted me to the end of the war. I had nothing else to wear. It was probably fortunate that I was so thin and small at this stage of the war, because the two tea towels barely fit me, using every inch of cloth."*

Phyllis's cut off hair, which she possesses to this day.

CHAPTER SEVEN

WISDOM

Moving House in Tjideng

After several months in Tjideng, we moved to the opposite end of the camp. This was not a problem, as we had so few belongings. What we owned in the way of bedding, along with our original little suitcase, could easily be carried. We were again crowded into a house with other women and children, including a variety of Asian women in their sarongs and bujas, about sixty of us in all. The barbed-wire fence was right behind our new house, and I could see the local people living their daily lives. I remember standing there and looking out at the men and women in their sarongs, with baskets on their head, walking to and from their village. Sometimes they walked beside donkeys that pulled carts or carried loads of sticks or crops in gunnysacks on their back. I wondered what life was like for these people in their village. They could see us, too—what did they think of our being prisoners behind barbed wire? I certainly knew I was a prisoner by this time, unable to visit them freely like we did before the war. Sometimes they would wave to us and we would wave back. It felt like a pleasant connection with the outside world, forbidden to us, except for the friendly wave and smile.

Mother: *"After about three months in the camp, the facility was reorganized and we were shifted to a new section. We realized that the Japanese had expanded the camp to include more houses that were part of the suburbs of Batavia. Rolls of barbed wire were positioned* beyond these houses to enclose them into Tjideng. Many of them still had some limited furnishings, remnants of curtains and household items, books and games abandoned by the Dutch who had lived there before the war. The houses even had flourishing gardens with hibiscus flowers and many varieties of tropical garden plants.

"The location of our new house was beyond a large, open-sided building with low walls, open at the top of the wall allowing you to see into the building and covered with an atap roof, so we were isolated from the rest of the housing by some distance. I figured that the large building might once have been an area for meetings or that it also could have been used as a marketplace, and that the isolated house on the far side was the home of the caretaker. Whatever the reason for the unusual setup, it was very fortunate for our household as it kept us far away from the rest of the camp, and we could be a little more at peace. All the atrocities dreamed up by Sonei took place in the central main street of the camp near the main gate, and we were far away from there now.

"All the Americans lived in the one house, and the Australians in a separate house near us on the other side of the large empty building. I've never quite figured out why the Australians weren't housed with the rest of the British, but that's how it was. Many Asian women who had married American men were also allocated to our new house. There were sixty of us and we were packed into a dwelling that normally held a family of four. There were two bedrooms, a sitting room, a kitchen, a bathroom, and a tiny study. We all had to fit into this house one way or another. Every inch of floor space was used for sleeping, even in the bathroom. We were required to do our own cooking in the limited facilities of the small family kitchen. Since the house had belonged to the Dutch before the war, the plumbing was European style with sinks and running water, as well as a regular flush toilet with a septic tank outside.

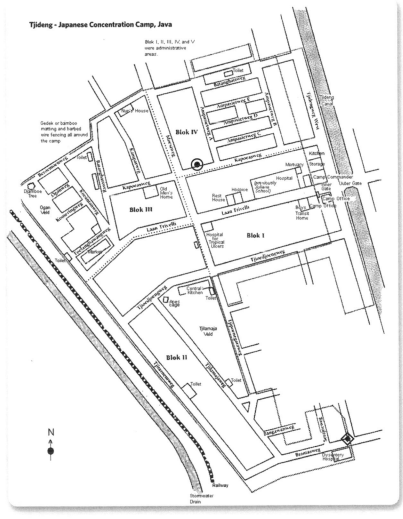

⊙ First house in Tjideng Camp   ◈ Second house in Tjideng Camp

"For some reason known only to them, the Japanese put me in charge of our American household and of the Australian household on the other side of the marketplace. I was the designated spokesperson for both groups, and I was also responsible for dividing food fairly. The raw food had to be collected daily from the main street near the camp entrance. This required about a fifteen-minute walk from our house, each way. The women thought I should cook the food for everyone as well as collect it. However, my first attempt to cook for so many people was viewed very poorly by everyone. I burned the rice and our precious rations were ruined. After that, the Asian women agreed to cook the food for all of us. They certainly did a far better job with what little we got to share.

"We were very lucky to have in our house a Burmese woman—married to an American—who had considerable knowledge of edible plants. Tjideng was the only camp we were ever in where anything grew. In the early hours of the morning, our housemate would wander through the streets of the neighboring houses and collect flowers, twigs, leaves, berries, and roots to add to our pot of rice. Occasionally, I accompanied her to collect hibiscus leaves. Collecting these plants was a very dangerous practice. If caught by any Japanese guard, we could be severely punished. Fortunately, we were on the outskirts of the camp and attracted little attention from the guards. It was also important to avoid comment from the other internees in other houses. We had several troublemakers in our midst who would have had no compunction about reporting us to the guards, in the hopes of getting favors for themselves. The Burmese woman was able to make her collection in a casual, unobtrusive way, stuffing the plants in the folds of her sarong or in a little flat basket under her skirt. There certainly was not enough foliage to provide for everyone in the camp. We were lucky to have this specialized knowledge to give us some much-needed vitamins and minerals that would help us stay a little healthier. We were the only group that didn't get edema badly. That's a sort of beriberi, which results from lack of the vitamin thiamine in the diet. The body breaks down and looks swollen. We certainly didn't get much in the way of nutritious food from the Japanese.

"Thankfully, none of us got skin ulcers or sores while living in this house, either. That's because we were able to keep clean. Something I had learned growing up in Hawaii was that the sap from hibiscus leaves, if steeped in water, is a very good cleansing agent and acts as an antiseptic. It served as a good substitute for soap. As a child playing out in the woods in Honolulu, I once met a Hawaiian woman washing her hair and I asked her what she used to clean it as I did not see any soap. She told me she soaked the hibiscus leaves in water and used the liquid to wash her hair. That memory surfaced from somewhere to serve us well in the camp. Also the frayed ends of hibiscus twigs served well as toothbrushes. There weren't too many hibiscus plants in the camp, but some grew where we lived in the newly enclosed area—although not enough to take care of fifteen thousand people, that's for sure. I secretly collected the leaves in the early morning, before tending to duties allotted to me by the Japanese. With the slimy water that accrued from soaking the torn leaves, we all washed our hair and our bodies, and the disinfectant properties helped us avoid skin diseases. So we were lucky that between the two of us, the Burmese woman and me, we had a little bit more knowledge than anybody else that kept us slightly better off.

This was another reason to feel fortunate that we were located beyond the main housing, out of sight of other households.

"When we arrived into this camp, we found the women were organized into three main work parties according to age. I am not sure whether the Japanese or the women had arranged this. Most of the internees we met in Tjideng had been there since the beginning of the war and had a fairly well organized system in place into which we had to fit. Those between eighteen and twenty-eight did all the heavy work— lifting rice sacks, unloading the bread trucks, running up barbed-wire fences, and similar legwork. The younger women who were on the heavy duties also kept gardens where food was grown for the hospital. None of this food was ever distributed to us in the camp. Those between twenty-eight and thirty-eight were what they called the hygiene crew. I was in that group. Those between thirty-eight and forty-eight took care of the sick. Anyone under eighteen and over forty-eight years of age did not work. The hygiene crew had four main jobs to do: one was cleaning the sewers; another was carrying the sick from their respective houses to the small hospital; one was making coffins, made of bamboo latched together with very coarse rope; and the other was carrying the dead onto the empty trucks after the bread had been taken off. As far as I know the trucks were never disinfected before being used for bread again. The bread came in, the bodies went out. I don't know where the bodies were taken. We were never told. Whether they were buried or not, and where, was a mystery.

"The reason the sewers had to be cleaned was because there wasn't really a sewage system as such. Each house had what was called a barefoot, or cesspool. As the house was built for four people, it obviously

wasn't going to cope with the troubles of sixty people. The sewers over-
flowed or got too full and had to be emptied by hand. We emptied them
into cans, scooping with half-coconut shells, and then had to carry the
cans outside the camp or to the gardens. Sometimes we were only able
to empty the sewer contents onto the road."

Donald and I stayed in the vicinity of the house during the times our mother performed her duties in the main street of the camp. Although separated from normal life outside the camp by the six-foot-deep, coiled barbed wire just beyond our house, as the weeks went by, we established bolder communication with the native passersby, even though this practice was highly dangerous. Donald frequently crawled through the rolls of wire to barter with the natives for food. He was very tiny for his age, nippy and agile, quick on his feet and in all his movements, that he easily managed the feat. He was never caught. I watched him do it sometimes, looking around to be sure there were no Japanese guards coming our way. For me standing by, the fear of Donald getting caught was tremendous, although I don't think he had any idea how risky his activity was. Often the women in the house would encourage him to trade on their behalf, giving him a piece of cloth to exchange for a papaya or banana. Our mother never knew of these activities, although she may have wondered where the extra fruit came from on occasion.

Donald was very lucky; a Dutch woman trading through the barbed wire near our house was not as fortunate. She was caught by a guard, who marched her off to Sonei's office. We later saw her with her head shaved. She told us it was a punishment for trading cloth for fruit through the fence.

Mother: *"After the war was over and we could walk freely through the local community, I found out from the other women in the camp that they had used Donald as a go-between to exchange cloth for fruit. It was just as well I didn't know because I would have had a fit and stopped it. Everyone kept it a big secret from me."*

On one occasion, I accompanied my mother to her work, which was cleaning the "madhouse." This was the market like place next to our house, a walled-in area now filled with beds. The tops of the walls were open to allow the breeze through and the atap roof overhung the walls so that any rain would fall away from the building and keep the inmates protected from the elements. Each patient was tied by her wrists to the frame of her bed. Most of the women behaved in peculiar ways, appearing to be very mad indeed, singing, shouting, calling out all sorts of nonsense, struggling against their tied wrists to try to free themselves. Nothing they said made sense. One woman constantly sang "Ave Maria" over and over again in the most beautiful voice. "It's enough to send everyone else crazy," my mother said. To this day she cannot stand to hear it. While my mother was cleaning this place, one of the women broke free from her wrist straps and ran frantically toward us. My mother grabbed my hand and managed to scramble us both over the wall in double-quick time, out of reach of the demented woman. The other woman on cleaning duty with my mother did the same. "Whew, that was a close call," my mother gasped as we tried to catch our breath and recover from our fright.

Games were few and far between, but I did have a set of jacks that materialized from somewhere in the camp. I was taught how to play and became quite adept at swishing up the correct number of jacks into my hand with one bounce of the little black ball. It also taught me to count in English, Dutch, and Japanese. I also played with the ball separately out on the road. When I missed catching it one day, it rolled into the sewer drain. I was devastated. My mother gallantly reached one arm into the drain to rescue my precious toy and found it in the mess of sewage. "Don't you dare lose it again," she said. "It will stay in the sewer next time." And indeed, I was much more careful after that.

On another occasion, I accompanied my mother to the main street of the camp, where the trucks drove in with our daily rations. The food was dumped in the middle of the street. My mother's duty that time was to make coffins. She tied bamboo poles together with rope to make a long box. You could still see through the slats when the coffin was finished. When the food had been unloaded from the trucks, those same trucks were then loaded with the coffins, each containing a dead body. Since all this work had to be done by the women in my mother's "hygiene crew," the coffins were loaded empty and then the dead bodies were lifted up onto the truck separately. One dead woman was too tall for the coffin and didn't fit. Her feet stuck out over the end. I watched a Japanese soldier hop onto the truck, break the legs of this corpse, snap them back at the knees, and fold them underneath the body so that the body could fit the box. No amount of protestation from the women over this grisly task made any difference to the Japanese. Meals were sparse. Raw rice was divided up equally among all the houses and each household had to cook its own portion and divide it up equally among everyone living in the house. The women who did all the cooking in our house had little to work with. A handful of cooked rice, some awful slimy seaweed substance called kankong, and a slice of sago bread were all each of us was given twice a day.

We were always hungry. Every now and then we'd get a pickled egg, which was delicious. My mother collected the eggshells from anyone who did not want theirs. She dissolved dozens of eggshells in water, creating a chalky liquid, and made Donald and me drink it. "This will give you calcium to grow strong bones," she told us.

Long loaves of bread were allocated to each house daily. My mother was given the job of dividing it fairly among everyone. We all gathered around to be sure that she did. She had a tape measure from somewhere and used it to measure off three inches of bread for each person. It was a daily ritual—measuring the bread equally and using a blunt knife to carefully saw through the loaf. One time, I broke a tooth, biting into my slice of bread. A long rusty nail was embedded in the slice. Fortunately, it was a tooth ready to fall out anyway, but it had been too painful to pull out, so I'd suffered with it half-dangling in my mouth. The nail took care of that.

Another time, I was accused of stealing someone's bread. I had not done so. My being questioned by my mother for some time to own up, with her telling me that I had been seen in the room where the bread had been stored and was therefore suspect, troubled me. In the end, my mother shared our three portions with the aggrieved victim to be sure she had something to eat that day, but she assured the woman that I was not the thief.

Mother: *"Our diet was indeed very meager. It got progressively less and less as the war dragged on. We got approximately three quarters of a teacup of cooked rice twice a day, and about three inches of so-*

called bread. Heaven alone knows what it was made of but I was told it was a kind of sago—a powdery starch made from processing pith found inside the trunks of the sago palm. The bread was reasonably soft when you got it, but there was no use keeping it for later because it got as hard as a brick and nobody could chew it, or do anything with it after it got hard. We also got soup made with a kind of grass in it called kankong. It tasted awful and I don't know whether it was good for you or not, but that's what we got. Once a fortnight, we were given chopped offal. That was the only thing I didn't share out absolutely equally with you. You got my share. And once a fortnight, not at the same time, we got an egg, usually a hard-boiled duck egg that was preserved in brine. It tasted very good. I gathered up all the shells from the people that were going to throw theirs away and mashed them up into a fine powder, put them in water, and gave it to you two children to drink, hoping you'd get a little bit of calcium out of that. That was our diet until the end of the war. When we did get out of Java and were taken to the hospital in Calcutta, I don't know what you children weighed, the doctor never told me, but I weighed in at seventy-two pounds. I had also shrunk an inch from five feet two inches to five feet one inch.

"During the evenings after you children were asleep, many of the women gathered together to talk about their lives before the war and reminisce about better times. A favorite pastime was to imagine a visit to a favorite restaurant. We would take turns describing the meal of our choice in detail, savoring the memory of the tastes and flavors. We enjoyed many an evening visiting a different restaurant each night. We were all so hungry all the time. We learned a great deal about different dishes and often learned how to cook certain recipes we had never *heard of. It was an escape and helped us through those difficult times. As the years wore on, it became increasingly difficult to stay alert and constructive. Something I tried to do daily was to see something beautiful, hear something beautiful, and say something beautiful or be of help to someone. When I saw a gorgeous sunset, of which there were many in Java, I would stop to admire it and say to myself, 'Thank you, that's my something beautiful to see for today.' It could be a hummingbird, a hibiscus flower, or a flower growing out of the dirt. Sounds of beauty included birdsong or laughter or the sounds of daily activities of the people beyond the barbed wire. 'Fancy, someone is actually laughing!' and I could smile, too. It was always easy to give an encouraging word to someone who was depressed under the circumstances, or offer an act of kindness to cheer someone up. We would give each other manicures using such water as we had, using trimmed sticks and old emery boards salvaged from the households abandoned by the Dutch, which were now our living quarters. A woman who requested having her hair and face done nicely usually died the next day. It seemed strange to know that a dying woman's request was to look nice in her last hours. No words of encouragement or determination on our part could change the woman's mind-set. The mood of the woman having her face and hair done was one of deep resignation and a lack of a will to live any more. The spirit and will to live was gone, and only the request to look nice remained. We always honored the request with sadness, doing the best job possible under the circumstances, offering love, care, and attention.*

"One of the worst duties I had to do in camp was to announce to any of the women in my house that her husband had died. I would be called to Sonei's office and given a package with the name of the man

who had died. The package contained a lock of hair and the finger-nails of the dead husband to be given to his widow. I think this had something to do with the Japanese custom of ancestor worship. If the package was for a woman in my house, it was my duty to give it to her and inform her that her husband was gone. Giving her the package was most unpleasant and slightly gruesome. The sadness and tears was often overwhelming. Fortunately, I myself never received such a package. There was hope that Frank was still alive."

I often played in the street with other children, but always looked out for my mother's returning home from her daily work duty. She spent many hours teaching me to read and write in English. Although I spoke Dutch fluently—it was the language I had settled on after being spoken to in so many tongues as a toddler—my mother taught me to read in English. Generally, our conversations consisted of my speaking to her in Dutch and my mother's replying in English. Three books were found in the last house we lived in. These were The House at Pooh Corner by A. A. Milne, and The Dutch Twins and The Norwegian Twins by Lucy Fitch Perkins. Fortunately, they were written in English. They must have been left behind in the houses when their owners escaped the island. The Japanese took everything in the way of books and writing equipment, so these books had to be hidden when they were around. My mother continued using a stick in the dirt to teach me words, but now my education included reading from the three books. It was a struggle to read them although I enjoyed their being read to me. My mother made every effort to teach me to read the books myself, having me repeat the words from the page. In this way, I slowly made progress. I finally managed to get through the whole of The Dutch Twins by myself. It was the simpler of the two "twin" books featuring five-year-old twins living in Holland. And I loved the Milne book—Christopher Robin and Winnie the Pooh were enchanting to me, especially the part where Pooh got stuck in the rabbit hole, and the rabbit used his legs as a towel rack.

In addition to reading aloud, my mother told us many stories of life in other lands and places she had visited. She painted vivid word pictures of Waikiki Beach, Diamond Head, coral seas, and colorful fish, recalling her childhood days of growing up in Honolulu, Hawaii. Pine forests, lochs, and heather moors described the Scottish scenery of my father's homeland. Her descriptions of skyscrapers in New York City intrigued me. I tried to imagine tall buildings beside streets so narrow that you could only see a little sliver of sky high up between them.

As for math, I eventually memorized the multiplication tables up to twelve. My mother's mathematical ability did not stretch much beyond that, although I did add, subtract, and multiply some simple sums.

This ad hoc schooling in the camps instilled us with a sense of purpose. Surviving in a concentration camp requires resilience and the ability to summon the spirit to get through each day, no matter what happens. For many of the interned women, illness, hatred, and a deep despondence became irreversible and undermined their will to live. Women who gave up showed it in their eyes, a listlessness and hopelessness emanating from their very being, although they often asked to have their hair combed, their faces made up, and their nails manicured. My mother, however, was a survivor. During those years she often said, "No Japanese is going to make me curl up my toes and die." She kept busy with her bridge games and her "favorite restaurant" games—and she focused on the future with a positive outlook. She told us stories of the beautiful places where she had lived before the war to educate us and cheer us up. But many of her other stories started with, "When the war is over...."

My mother told me when the war was over, I would go to school and go to University. She ingrained this concept into my mind. If anyone asked me what I was going to do when I grew up I said, "I am going to university," not that I had any inkling of what that meant. My mother described it to me as a place where I would meet many people in beautiful large buildings with lecture rooms, where professors would teach me about anything I wanted to know. It seemed marvelously mysterious to me and I was certain I would go to one when I grew up.

Indeed, back in England a few years later, I would manage to secure the one open spot in a particular grammar school in Essex, by assuring Miss Leworthy, the imposing headmistress, during my admissions interview that, when I grew up, "I was going to university." And indeed I did study for a degree in Geography at University College, London University, after I left school. In later years when I practiced meditation, I learned the ancient teaching, "What you hold in consciousness is your own self-fulfilling prophecy." How true! The Dalai Lama constantly exhorts his listeners to "cultivate the imagination" despite the trials and tribulations of life, and to try again and again, no matter what happens. In retrospect, my mother prepared me well for life, even within the confines of a Japanese concentration camp. What is it about the mind that can see beyond the confines of barbed wire and prison walls to view a life rich with possibilities—and to imbue that image of hope and a better future into the mind of a child?

THE MISSIONARY LADY

Many of the women in the household listened to my mother's stories while she was teaching Donald and me, enthralled by her fund of information and vivid stories. They frequently told her how much they enjoyed listening to her and that they learned so much, too.

But one older woman who lived in our house was very odd. She was plump and round, a big woman to me, and a little overpowering. She behaved strangely toward us children, always trying to get us to sing religious songs or telling us stories about Jesus. She would gather a group of children together in front of our house and teach Bible stories. She gave us pictures illustrating Bible stories, if we attended her Sunday school classes. These seemed to take place every day. We sang doleful hymns. After two or three attendances, I refused to go any more, her gift of little pictures notwithstanding! I did not like her at all, and avoided her company around the house whenever possible.

Mother: *"This old missionary lady, probably in her mid seventies, was placed in the American household when she was transferred to our camp. As she had American nationality, she was put in my charge. She originally came from New York. As a member of the Salvation Army, she had been stationed in Borneo with the Dyaks for the best part of fifty years. I think the Salvation Army forgot they sent her there and never took her home again. The Japanese found her there and brought her into our camp. She was a simple woman, lost in her religious world. I did have occasion to stop her from inserting her own words to the hymns or songs she taught the children. Her using words like, 'My father has gone off to war / My father may never come back,' to the tune of 'My Bonnie Lies over the Ocean' upset me terribly. I forbade her to use such words to influence the children's minds negatively about their fathers and to only sing the accepted words for hymns and songs. My anger must have gotten through to her because she never repeated that episode again, to my knowledge.*

"Toward the end of the war, the Japanese allowed six telegrams to be sent from the camps to anywhere in the world. Of course, with the thousands of people, it was difficult to know who would use the telegrams. It was finally decided that one could be sent from our American-Australian group; one from the British group; one from the Dutch East Indies' governor-general's wife, Mrs. Tjarde Van Starkenborg Stachouwer; and three would be divided up amongst the Dutch. We decided to draw lots to decide who could send the telegram from our group. The old missionary lady got the telegram. 'Whom will you send it to?' I asked her. 'To my brother in New York,' she replied. 'That's good,' I said. 'He'll be pleased to hear from you and know that you are alive. As soon as you've written it, I'll take it around to Sonei's office.' This I did. Having been reasonably well brought up, I did not read her letter before I took it to Sonei's office. On the way back from the office, I dawdled around some friend's houses catching up with any news, so that by the time I got near our little house, I was astonished to see the missionary being frog-marched up the road with a number of guards pointing bayonets at her. I stopped to ask what the trouble was. 'She *has to be taken to Sonei,' one of the guards informed me. 'I'd better come along, too, to see what this is all about,' I responded. Since I was nominally in charge of her, I thought I'd better accompany her.*

"The interpreter told me when I got there that Sonei was convinced she had written a military code in her telegram. Instead of sending the telegram to her brother, she'd written it to the Salvation Army. Well, I don't suppose Sonei had ever heard of the Salvation Army and as far as he was concerned army was the operative word. Her telegram read, 'I'm scrubbing floors to the glory of God, Hallelujah!' and signed her name. Well, as I wasn't having any lady in her seventies scrubbing any floors, that was a lie to start with, and whatever possessed her to write this I'll never know. I told the interpreter that the Salvation Army was a religious organization, not a military one. And that just precisely what she meant by her message, I didn't know, but she was a little bit not right in the head and probably didn't realize what she was doing. Based on this explanation, the interpreter took me before Sonei to plead her case. I did such a good job that he let her loose and told me that he would have me there as a spy instead and he would kill me instead of her. That's when I really started talking. Fortunately the interpreter had been educated in America and understood the situation very well and was able to convince Sonei of my story. The interpreter finally turned to me and said, 'Leave quickly; Sonei said to get you out of here. You'd better go before he changes his mind.' So somehow I talked my way out of that one, and here I am to tell the tale. I never really forgave the missionary lady for the fright she gave me. She did survive the war and was sent back to New York, but I don't know what happened to her."

THE THREE-MONTH STRATEGY

Days and weeks passed in routines of work, food allocations, and evening stories. We felt progressively hungrier with less and less energy to do anything much, as the third year of our internment passed and we were well into our fourth year. My mother told me years later that one of her survival tactics as the war lingered on without her having any idea when it was to end, was to imagine that she could live through the next three months under the present conditions we were in. Three months seemed like a manageable amount of time to survive the present conditions. She said she could always visualize herself being able to do that each day through three and half years, a continuously flowing series of three months.

Meanwhile, I was having problems with some of the boys my age following me around and taunting me. This was exacerbated by my bandana, which I stubbornly continued to wear after my hair had been shorn, and the boys loved to tease me about it.

One time, I had climbed up onto a pile of dirt to get away from them when they started to throw stones at me, taunting me to come down so that they could take my bandana off. Just at this moment, Donald showed up and launched a blistering attack on the three boys, all arms and legs kicking and screaming at them to leave me alone, distracting their attention away from me and allowing me to escape. Although my brother does not remember much of the camp years, he certainly remembers this event, frequently reminding me of the day he rescued me from a stoning! He was almost six at the time.

The End of the War

Toward the end of the war, just before my ninth birthday, the Japanese provided the camp with more freely running water from hoses on certain days of the week. My mother insisted on bathing Donald and me out in the open sunshine, spraying the water over us. My exposed nakedness bothered me immensely and I protested vehemently about being out in the open for everyone to see. It did not bother my mother one little bit, however; she only laughed at my embarrassment. "It's good to have fresh water and to be out in the sunshine to dry," she said. A gang of boys gathered round at the commotion and laughed at us, pointing fingers at us. I was mortified and felt a distinct sense of modesty flood over me during the experience.

When my ninth birthday rolled around on the August 1, 1945, there was very little to provide for a celebration. By this time food restriction was severe, and there was little extra to provide for any kind of party. A few hibiscus flowers and everyone singing "Happy Birthday" in both Dutch and English had to suffice.

CHAPTER EIGHT

JOY

LIBERATION

Several weeks after my ninth birthday, things changed. The gates of the camp were opened one day—and left open. All the Japanese guards disappeared, and we were in the camp on our own. It was the first time we could leave the camp freely. We traded overtly with the local people, giving them bits of cloth in exchange for food. But, "We have to wait until help arrives," my mother told us. "We have no means to get ourselves anywhere and we have to find Daddy before we can leave."

The head of the local Chinese Kong came into the camp and offered his services. If there was anything we needed, he would try to help us. The women were too debilitated to know what to ask for, except for any food the Kong could spare.

It was several days before uniformed men, mostly British and Dutch officials, arrived and placed tables in the street, to process prisoners-of-war of those nationalities. Meanwhile, American officials set up an office in town, where my mother had to register us. The secret American passport, hidden in my frilly bloomers all those years during tenko, finally came into the light and established her nationality.

Mother: *"A hidden radio kept secret from the Japanese informed us that the war was ended with the atomic bombs dropped on Hiroshima on August 6, 1945, and three days later on Nagasaki. A group of women went up to Sonei and told him the news. None of the Japanese* seemed to know that the war had ended and continued to keep guard over us for many days after those momentous events. After they confirmed what had happened, they all quietly left the camp, leaving the gates wide open.

"We now had to wait and see what would happen to us next, as we had no means of taking ourselves anywhere. Help soon came in the form of Allied officials who inspected our camp. We felt very relieved to see them, the first Western men we'd laid eyes on in three and a half years. I was told that the American officials had set up office in the main town of Batavia and I had to go there to register my existence.

"There were few people in the office, but one person in the American Allies' office was Lady Mountbatten, head of the Red Cross at that time. She was looking for two children who had been separated from their parents at the start of the war. The children belonged to one of the British consulate staff; their parents were alive in Singapore. I knew exactly who these children were, as two New Zealand nurses in my section of the camp had—for all practical purposes—adopted them when the ship taking them to Australia was sunk at the beginning of the war. This news enabled Lady Mountbatten to bring about a happy family reunion. It was to be the first of many.

"When I presented myself as an American with a U.S. passport in hand, having carefully hidden it from the Japanese throughout the war, the American official told me, 'We'll take you out as soon as possible to wherever you want to go.'

"'That is wonderful,' I replied, 'but first I must find out where my husband is located and bring him here. I am not leaving the island without him.' But when I told the U.S. officials that my husband was

British, they said they were not permitted to find him. However, if I could find him, they would repatriate us together as a family to anywhere in the world. I had to think about a solution to this problem. How could I find Frank in the whole of Java?"

The newly arrived uniformed men organizing everything were friendly, neat, and trim. The American soldiers handed out chewing gum and sweets. All of a sudden, life became very exciting. All the action and friendly smiles gave us all a sense of hope for the future. Our hungry minds and bodies changed quickly. Food arrived, and the Americans brought in a huge movie screen that towered over us all in the main street, where they showed films in the evening. The first movie I ever saw was outdoors in the main street of the camp. It was The Wizard of Oz, with Judy Garland. I was enchanted. It was a magical and delightful experience. I thrilled to the movie's music and color, and the "yellow brick road," and will never forget it. Starlit nights, more food, movies out in the street at night—this was a whole new experience of life. In the meantime, my mother was trying to figure out how to locate my father.

Mother: *"I remembered the Chinese community in Tjepoe. Before the war, the head of the Kong had told me to ask for any help I might need at any time, and then, any member of the Kong would give me whatever I required. Now, the head of the local Chinese Kong had come into our camp after the Japanese left and offered to help us. But none of us knew what to ask for, except for any food they could spare. Once I knew what to ask for, I went to the local head of the Kong in Batavia and asked if he could find Frank.*

"'Write a letter to your husband explaining your situation. If he is alive, we will find him and bring him to you in two days,' the Kong leader told me. There was no question that he was serious. He put the letter into the hands of a member of his community with strict instructions to find Frank Nisbet, and to personally hand Mr. Nisbet my letter and tell him to come to Tjideng camp.

"Daddy walked into the camp two days later with Auntie Vena. She had seen Frank in town and brought him back to our camp. Vena's son Ron, seeing Frank beside his mother, ran excitedly up to him with his arms waving, shouting, 'Daddy, Daddy,' thinking this was his own father. It was the saddest thing I ever saw when Ron was told that Frank was not his daddy but Phyllis and Donald's daddy. The look of sheer disappointment and dejection in little Ron's face and body was heartbreaking."

"That is your daddy," my mother told me, pointing to the tall, very thin man walking in through the gates of our camp. I felt overwhelmed. Seeing Ron's exuberant welcome and subsequent disappointment, I held back a little before running up to my father and getting a big hug. It was wonderful. At last, all the stories my mother told of us all being together again one day were now coming true. We all felt very emotional, expressing amazement that we were all alive and together again. Auntie Vena, however, had not been able to track down her husband, Martin. He was a missing person.

We had to say good-bye to Auntie Vena and Ron when the Americans arranged for us to leave Java and be taken back to England.

Mother: "We were flown out of Java on our tenth wedding anniversary, the twenty-fifth of September 1945. The American repatriation *officials first took us to Singapore and then transferred us to another plane to Calcutta, where we were put in the American Red Cross hospital. We stayed there to be given checkups and medical treatment. Daddy had a very advanced stage of beriberi and severely blurred eyesight. I only weighed seventy-two pounds. We both needed good nutrition and mega-vitamin shots, especially vitamin B. The doctors warned us not to eat too much too quickly, but I desperately craved food. The first meal I requested was a big plate of bacon and eggs. After three days, I was discharged from the hospital and we were housed in Lady Mountbatten's Red Cross headquarters in Calcutta. This was a very large house. Its many rooms were filled with Red Cross packages from all over the world—the packages were stacked from floor to ceiling. I was told that if I could find any clothes in any of them to fit us, that we could have them. I was still dressed in my tea-cloth bikini. It was a discouraging task trying to find clothes that fit. Kind people from all over the world had knitted all sorts of things and sent clothes they no longer needed, to give to 'poor refugees.' I ended up with an outsize cotton dress for me and a huge pair of trousers for Frank, which he had to keep on with rope tied through the belt loops since I could not find a belt in any of the parcels I opened. I managed to find fairly suitable outfits for the two of you children that fit reasonably well."*

The journey was very exciting. I loved it. We flew first to Singapore and then again to Calcutta in a wide-bellied paratrooper military plane with a spacious interior and benches along it's inside wall. It was during this flight that I had my first experience of seeing the earth's surface from the window of an airplane. Running from window to window, I spent hours looking out at the ground far below. As we flew in to Calcutta, my mother pointed out the Brahmaputra River and Ganges delta, clear as crystal, with the Brahmaputra's distinctive rectangular pattern and the delta's braiding as the two rivers joined together and entered the ocean. From above I could see how the rivers joined each other, one turning sharply around the mountain ranges, the other on a vast flat plain. I've never forgotten it. We stayed in Calcutta so that my parents could be treated in an American Red Cross Hospital for several weeks. Time just flew by. Donald and I had a very good time. The American GIs adopted us, the first Western children they had seen in a long time. They took turns treating us to rides around town in their jeeps. Donald even rode on the back of a motorbike, hanging on for dear life as a GI took him out "just for fun." Donald loved the speed and excitement. "Which do you prefer, Donald, airplanes or jeeps?" my father asked, "Jeeps." "Why?" "They go faster," came the unhesitating reply.

We stayed in the hospital for the first three days in Calcutta and then moved to a big house filled with packages. We had fun opening them, trying to find clothes for ourselves. We found lots of baby clothes, little knitted hats and small sweaters. It took us a long time to find something that we could wear.

Mother: *"When Daddy could see again and we were released from the Red Cross Hospital, the Americans transferred us to the British section for repatriation to Great Britain. The British authorities told the Americans that they could only transport military personnel. All they had were military planes, and no civilians were allowed to fly in them. To get around this, the British created temporary military positions for us as a family. Daddy was flown out as a general, I was a lieutenant,*

Phyllis and Donald at the Red Cross Hospital in Calcutta, 1945

and you two children were our batmen! We were given all the official documents to show this. I pleaded with the authorities when we got to England to allow us to keep the papers, but they wouldn't since it had been a highly irregular solution to repatriate us quickly. Nevertheless, it was a very interesting experience.

"We left by flying boat and had quite an eventful journey back to Britain, stopping in Karachi for refueling and again in Alexandria, and finally in Sicily, the last because something fell off the plane and we had to land there and stay until they could get parts out from England. We had a most enjoyable week in Sicily. We were treated to daily pasta feasts with delicious sauces, on the dockside near where the plane had landed in the water. Servings of locally baked breads and a wide variety of cheeses and fresh fruits accompanied these meals. The weather was perfect and the people most hospitable and kind. Finally, another plane came out for us. The pilot of that replacement plane was very interested that we hadn't heard about the Normandy landings. So he very kindly went out of his way and flew us over the Normandy beaches and explained it all to us, showing us where everything had happened when the invasion of Europe took place. The seaplane landed in Poole harbor in the south of England.

"Returning safely back to England felt to us like some sort of miracle. That we were all together and reasonably well was a blessing. Aunty Vena was not so lucky. She stayed in Java for another two years, trying to find out if her husband, Martin, was still alive. Eventually she found out he had been transported with a group of European doctors as POWs to be taken to Japan to serve in Japanese military hospitals. Unfortunately, our allies bombed and sank the ship, and Martin died along with everyone else on it. Vena finally returned to England with Ron and eventually remarried. We always kept in touch over the years and remained very good friends. She died a few years ago of breast cancer. I was deeply saddened by her death, as she was a really good friend and a dear woman.

"As for Mrs. Nordhoekhecht, who protected you children the night of Sonei's dog-killing rampage, I have often wondered what happened to her. Unfortunately, I do not know. In the excitement of meeting Daddy and leaving the island, I could have kicked myself afterward for not mentioning to the American authorities who repatriated us that her son had been killed in service at Pearl Harbor. Surely they would have helped her get home to Holland? Perhaps they did, if she mentioned her son to them. Many a time, I have regretted not doing so myself."

Father: "We traveled first to London for me to report back to Shell House, the headquarters of the Shell Oil Company in the middle of London. We stayed in a hotel in London for two days so that I could have time to present myself to the director of the company. His first words to me were not very welcoming. He said, 'Why are you here in England before Mr. Austin, the director of the refinery in Tjepoe?' 'The Americans brought my family here. My wife is an American,' I explained. Needless to say, he did not seem very pleased that I had returned before my supervisor! I said that I hoped to get my job back with the company as soon as possible, as I had a family to support. I added that first I would be visiting my mother in Scotland for a reunion, since I had not seen her or my family for over seven years. He asked me to report back to London the following the week. In the meantime, he assured me, they would figure out a position for me."

While my father was away, Donald and I were kept busy in our hotel room with colored pencils and coloring books. Our mother had bought large picture books with black outlines of pictures that we had to fill in. I remember the activity well, along with the cool October air outside when we took breaks and walked out of the hotel. I was not used to cold air, and even inside the hotel room it was fairly chilly. We all wore warm clothes, another unusual experience for us.

Mother: *"We traveled from London to Edinburgh on the Flying Scotsman. Gran (Frank's mother) and Auntie Joey (Frank's sister) were to meet us at the train station in Edinburgh. The Shell Company paid for our train tickets and we traveled first class. It was in the days when the trains had separate compartments in each carriage. Daddy, you, Donald, and I took up the seats facing each other. Somewhere along between London and Edinburgh, a Polish officer got on and sat opposite Donald. The officer was a very polite gentleman, tall and upright, and looked very proper in his uniform. Donald was so tiny, since he had not grown one inch the entire time we were in the camps and was the size of a three-year-old instead of a six-year-old; when he sat on the seat, his feet stuck straight out. The officer looked at Donald very directly for some time. Finally he smiled at Donald and said, 'Hello, little boy. And what's your name?' Well, by God that was the first time anybody had asked him that. He'd been saying it for three years and nobody had ever asked him before. Instantly, Donald recited his whole lineage right through, just as I had taught him in the camps. Daddy and the Polish officer looked so astounded, their eyes popping out, that I burst out laughing. We all got a good laugh once I explained the why of it. They both agreed that was a very sensible thing to have done. Donald was that pleased that somebody had actually asked him. His little face beamed. I was secretly very pleased that my strategy had worked so well—Donald came out pat, didn't miss a word. It was great. I was so proud of him."*

Our welcome from Gran was tremendous. She rolled out the proverbial red carpet for us. We had to take another train from Edinburgh to North Berwick, and the parade up the hill to Gran's home overlooking the Firth of Forth was a welcome second to none. She had the local people of the town out in force to greet us with ticker tape and welcome signs. It more than made up for the non-welcome my father had received at the Shell headquarters! We were the talk of the town: Isabella Nisbet's son and his family returned from a Japanese concentration camp, safe and sound. To be at the center of such attention was overwhelming. I felt like Dorothy on the yellow brick road in The Wizard of Oz, but this was me and my family being welcomed home by my grandmother and all her friends.

It was a beautiful autumn day, the sun shone, and I felt awed by the occasion of all these people coming out to greet us with such excitement. This would herald the start of a whole new life.

CHAPTER NINE

FATHER

My Father's Story

After my father was taken away in a truck in 1942, I did not see him again for over three years until he walked through the gates in Tjideng, when my mother pointed him out to me and said, "That's your daddy." During the postwar years, as I tried to catch up with my education and live a fairly normal family life in Essex and Scotland, I would occasionally hear snippets about my father's experiences in the camps he had been sent to. Usually he told of amusing occurrences that touched on the foibles of people of different nationalities. But apart from this, he rarely spoke of that time; it remained a mystery to me. I vaguely knew he had been in solitary confinement at some point, but he would not speak of it. Only when I finally got the tape from my parents did I hear his account of those war years. His soft, inimitable Scottish accent and occasional dry humor lilts through his story.

Father: *"When I was picked up in Bandoeng and taken away from you, the Japanese guard marched me outside the house and stuck a bayonet into my back, forcing me to the truck outside the gate, and indicated I should climb up. I joined a lot of fellows on there and was handcuffed to one of them. We went off in the dark and picked up quite a few more men, and were eventually taken to a building. I imagine it was a large school. We were crowded into one big classroom. Then they started shouting out the names again from the sheet of paper. As the* names were shouted out and the people went forward, they were taken away. We didn't, of course, know where we were going. But we just had to wait until our names were shouted out. Eventually this happened to me, and I was taken away and put into a truck with a lot of the people whose names had been called before mine. As soon as the truck was full, off we went.

"We were taken to a prison called Sukamiskin and marched in. Built by the Dutch, it was used from the late 1920s as a prison for Indonesian nationalists and was known to the people as a symbol of colonial suppression. Sukamiskin was a Sing Sing–like place, a traditional prison with rows of prison cells for hardened criminals like the kind you see in films. Each of us was stood in front of one of the doors and then told to get inside, where the doors were banged shut on us. I'll never forget that banging sound; it reminded me of the old saying, 'All you who have sinned, enter here.'

Sukamiskin Prison, Bandoeng

"We were in that prison for twenty-two months. The first six months were pretty terrible because we were each in solitary confinement. We were being punished for the way the Japanese had been treated by the Dutch when they were taken from Java to Australia, so the Japanese said. After about eight months, an important Japanese officer arrived and met with all of us in one big room. He talked in Malay. He told us that in future we would be treated like internees. From that time on until the end of the twenty-two months, we did have a lot more freedom inside the prison. We were allowed out of the cells about eight o'clock in the morning and weren't closed in again until eight o'clock at night.

"At the end of twenty-two months in this real prison, we were transferred to internment camps. They took us all out of the prison cells and loaded us up into trucks, which had blinds on them. We weren't allowed to see out and, of course, nobody could see in. We were taken away to what had been native barracks, a place called Chimahee. They were very extensive barracks, and in that camp there were about ten thousand of us, all men, packed in together. The British and Americans had a barracks of their own, separated from the Dutch who were in their own barracks.

"We thought that we had been pretty badly off in prison, but when we got to the internment camps, we realized we had been very, very well off indeed because, in these camps, there were absolutely no facilities whatsoever. We slept on concrete floors. I think we had about a meter each on the floor and no bedding at all. We just had to sleep on this very, very hard floor. Eventually, however, we did manage somewhere or other to get little strips of bedding and that made it just a little more comfortable. There were one hundred and twenty-eight people in my barrack. I was supposed to be in charge of them. That is to say, I was responsible for distributing food and seeing that the whole barrack was kept clean and tidy. The main thing, of course, was the distribution of food, which was very scarce. In the mornings, we got some stuff that was like billposter [billboard] paste for breakfast, along with a little square of so-called bread. I think the 'bread' was made with tapioca powder. Although it was quite soft when we received it, if you kept it for an hour it got very hard and was impossible to break. You couldn't really eat it; you just had to wolf it as soon as you got it. In addition to that, we got a mug of coffee—black coffee, no sugar, no milk. At midday, they let us have some liquid they called soup. It was mostly water with green leaves of some sort boiled up in it. In the evening we had soup again, with rice and very little else. Rice and watery soups were the mainstays of our daily diet. We had no meat at all and, after a while, quite a number of men started getting edema. Their legs swelled up and when the swelling actually got up as far as the stomach, they soon died.

"One time, the doctors among us in the camp advised us to catch rats, if possible. The people who had edema very badly used to skin these rats, boil them up, and eat their flesh. There was one Irishman with us, called Edwards. He got edema very badly. He was taken to the hospital and given a rat to eat. Afterward, he said, 'You know I've always heard these stories about these poor people in places like Leadersmith prison in England having to eat rats. Why? It's the most delicate flavor!'

"The question of feeding ten thousand involved quite a business in Chimahee camp. In fact, the cookhouses were like factories. About one hundred and fifty Dutch men ran them—until it was found that they were stealing a lot of our food. They were put out of the kitchen, and the eighty Chinese prisoners took over, after they had taken a vow to the headman that they would be honest and not steal any food. I must say that after they took over, things went a little better. We did occasionally get a little bit of pork. There wasn't enough meat to hand out to everyone so they cut it up into little squares and put it into the soup.

"The pork became something of a controversy. We had a number of Jews with us, including one in my section. It was arranged that when we had this soup with pork, that they would sit separately and get soup without pork. The first time we got pork, this worked out very well. Then, about a month later, we got pork again and the elderly Jew in my barrack lined up with us. He didn't like the soup that the Jews got. He had a brother in the camp and his brother was passing by as we were dishing out our soup. The brother shouted in consternation, 'Oh, Joseph, Joseph, you cannot eat that. It is pork, it is pork!' Instantly Joseph replied, 'When I am eating it, I will say, 'It is beef, it is beef, and it will be beef!'

"Another man in our camp always took his portion of food and ate it very slowly. He believed in chewing his food thoroughly and did so—up to fifty times for each mouthful. Of all the men in the camp, he was the only one I knew who never got stomach pains, diarrhea, or intestinal troubles. Perhaps there was something to the belief that if you chewed your food fifty times before swallowing each mouthful, you would stay healthy. He certainly was living proof of it. For the rest of us, we were always too hungry and lacking in discipline to eat that slowly, and usually wolfed our little portion of food down quickly, undoubtedly to our detriment health-wise.

"Several of the men in the camp were amazing traders. Starting off with nothing, they ended up after three and a half years in the camps with a tremendous hoard of goods. Somehow they had tricked other men through exchanges, betting, favors, and the like to part with their few precious possessions. It always intrigued me that this mentality persisted under such dire conditions.

"We were about ten months together in Chimahee camp. Then they told us that a number of us were to be shifted to another camp. How they picked the people that were going to the other camp, I don't know. But anyway, I was one of them. Two thousand of us were told to wrap all our things in straw matting and tie them up so they could be taken to the next camp. We didn't have to take anything with us; we just had to march. It took about an hour and a half of marching in the hot midday sun for us all to reach a camp they called Barris, and it was there that I spent the rest of the war. Conditions in the Barris camp were exactly the same as in the Chimahee camp, except that it was much smaller. I didn't have any duties there. We had just one fellow who seemed to be in charge of the British section. We were in a little barrack away from the Dutch; we didn't have much contact with them at all. The fellow that I said was in charge of the British section had been elected by the British men to represent them on the committee running the camp. He saw the head Dutchman every day and brought back any instructions that came from the Japanese to our barrack. From him I learned there was a camp nearby that was set aside as the central hospital for all the camps in the district. In it they had a hidden radio. The people who left the various camps to go out on work parties were able to contact fellow prisoners from the hospital camp and get the news. They, in turn, brought the news back to the various camps. The head of the camp passed it on.

"Apart from the size, there was one other difference between the Barris camp and the Chimahee camp. There was a man at Barris who had been a market gardener and he somehow or other managed to get seeds and plant tomatoes. He also got sweet potatoes, and soon had the whole place growing tomatoes and sweet potatoes. As soon as the plants bore fruit, the Japanese decided we had enough fresh food in the camp and they didn't send in any more vegetables at all. I don't know what happened to all the tomatoes, but we never saw any of them, either, and when we asked, we were told that they were reserved for sick people in the hospital. Now, I knew several people who had been to the hospital and none of them ever got tomatoes, either, so I think there was a little bit of jiggery-pokery going on somewhere.

"While I was at Barris, the Japanese brought in three young fellows. I don't know what they'd been doing, but they were brought to our camp to be punished. The Japanese method of punishment was to build cages out in the open and put each prisoner into one. These cages were made of wooden slats open to the weather. They left the three men inside their separate cages for about three days in the tropical sun. They couldn't sit down; they had to stand all the time. At the end of three days, when they were taken out, they were practically on their knees, unable to stand or walk. We were forced to witness this, but were never able to talk to these fellows to find out what had happened. The Japanese took them away again.

"We heard that the war had ended through the secret radio via the hospital. The camp gates were opened and the Japanese left. Soon the Allied authorities came into Barris to sort out citizens from their countries: Dutch, British, American, and Australian.

"One day, I received your mother's letter. Apparently the British military personnel at the main gate tried to take the letter from the Chinese man who had brought it, but he refused to hand it over to anyone except Frank Nisbet, as he had been instructed. When I read the contents I realized that I had to get permission to leave the camp, because our instructions were to stay put for the time being. We all knew, of course, that the war was over, but these were the instructions. So I had to get permission from the British repatriation people to leave my camp to go down to Batavia, as Jakarta was called in those days. This took a day or two. I eventually found a gentleman called Major Eggleston and explained the situation to him. He sat back and looked at me and said, 'You mean to tell me the Americans will take you out if I give permission?' I said, 'Yes, that's the situation.' And he said, 'Well, Frank, you're on your way.' With my permit in hand, I walked out of the camp and got on a train. I've never seen such a crowded train in my life. But we eventually arrived in Batavia and, after making a few inquiries, I found out where the women's camp was. It was a pretty long walk from the main central part of town. I was walking along this road when a car passed me. I stuck my thumb out to hitch a lift. A young woman got out, came dashing toward me, and threw her arms around me and kissed me. That was Auntie Vena. She was on her way to the Tjideng camp from her own camp, to visit with the three of you. I jumped in the car with her and we made our way to Tjideng.

"When Vena and I reached Tjideng and I walked into the camp with her, the first person to fling himself into my arms was little Ron crying, 'Daddy, Daddy.' It was a heartbreaking moment when he was told that I was not his daddy.

"The sight of my own wife, so tiny and thin with enormous eyes looking at me in wonder after so many terrible years, and my own two children so thin, yet running towards me with happy smiles was indeed an over-whelming moment for us all. The next problem was how to get out of the country, but you were there for that part of the story."

My father died in May 1991 at the age of eighty-six. He had been tested two years previously for disabilities related to his internment years and was awarded full medical benefits by the British government's military doctor in Gibraltar. His digestion was always a problem throughout the postwar years. In his seventies, he was finally diagnosed as having a slow version of tuberculosis in the peritoneum. An old doctor in Madrid, familiar with the condition from the World War I soldiers he had treated, recognized it. A ghastly medicine was prescribed that cured the condition; although my father suffered terribly from its side effects for several days after taking the drug it got rid of the TB, and he went on to live more healthfully for another fifteen years. An avid golfer all his life, he finally had to give up his beloved game when his eyesight deteriorated so that he could not see out of the lower quadrant of his vision. He was blind from the range of "four o'clock to eight o'clock," as he put it. This blindness was caused by a deterioration of the optic nerve and attributed to poor diet during the concentration camp years. Unable also to drive, he lost the two activities he loved the most. His physical inactivity resulted in a gradual decline in his health although he was never seriously ill, until he finally died in his sleep.

My mother recently revealed to me the emotional effects of the war years on my father.

Mother: *"He was never the same man I married and knew from before the war. Something terrible happened to him during those war years, where the life was knocked out of him. He must have gone deeply inside of himself, because he rarely asked for emotional help and was always very stoical. Two days after our reunion in Tjideng Camp, Frank said to me, 'Dorothy, you will have to bring up the children on your own; I have no strength or ability to do so. I will provide for the family, but that is all I can manage.' I was horrified and protested, saying that we had both gone through a terrible time and that we must work together to bring up our children. Frank just closed down, and I realized that he was not going to speak about the war years. I had to agree that it was best left behind us, that we had to move on with our lives as best we could, and so we never spoke about the war years to each other again. Your father just would not speak about his experience and he did not want to know what happened to us. Only when you asked questions about those experiences forty years later, was he willing to tell his experience. But even then he never touched on any of the true horrors that affected him deeply. He died with those secrets unlocked."*

I was deeply moved by my mother's revelation of my father's reaction to the war years. My memory of him, as I grew up in England, is of a quiet man, rarely participating in family decisions, happy to go along with what my mother planned.

Who knows how my father's life would have turned out had he not been imprisoned by the Japanese? He was born in 1904 in Leith, a port and suburb of Edinburgh, the son of a tailor of men's fashions who "had to marry" my grandmother five months before his child's birth. When my father was five, his father was tragically killed, by falling off a train while coming home from work. As was the local custom, people often opened the door of their compartment in anticipation of the train stopping at the platform, but my grandfather misjudged that day, thinking he was on the "stopping train" (the local) when actually he was on the nonstop (express) train. After this, my father's widowed mother, left to care for my father and his three-year-old sister, found work "in service" to a wealthy family in Edinburgh, which also provided her with a home for her young family. When the owners returned to England, they gave my grandmother a large severance to help her set up her own business. She bought a small shop with a combined post office and general store in the thriving suburbs of North Berwick.

My father grew up in this place overlooking the Firth of Forth and a nearby golf course. He learned to play golf at an early age and by eighteen became the local club champion. He gained a place at Edinburgh University to study chemistry and earned his first job with the Shell Oil Company to work in Mexico City. His mother, who by then was considered a wealthy woman, paid for all the fees for the university, but my father repaid every penny within the first five years of his work in Mexico.

He made many good friends through Shell during those years in Mexico, playing golf regularly and winning many tournaments. It was in Mexico City that he met my mother at an expatriate gathering. They were married within three weeks of meeting each other, in September 1935, and I was born eleven months later in Tampico.

When the Mexican government appropriated the oil fields in 1938, our family had to quit the country immediately, leaving behind most of their possessions in their Shell-provided house within the refinery, now also the possession of the Mexican government. My parents lost all their furnishings and equipment and many wedding gifts, taking with them only what they could pack in suitcases and steamer trunks. Fortunately, this did include most of my father's golf trophies made of Mexican silver.

My father was transferred by Shell to work in Borneo, subsequently to Java, to manage paraffin wax plants in Balikpapan, and then to Tjepoe. My brother was born in Tjepoe on July 4, 1939, when I was almost three years old, and it was there where we lived when Pearl Harbor was attacked on December 7, 1941. Our war-years ordeal began shortly after.

How sad that I did not really know my father. We had a powerful silent connection, however, and he was always very positive toward me. Perhaps his quiet support, along with my mother's energetic input, gave me confidence to try out new things and experience as much as possible. "Whatever you decide to do, we will help you," my father once offered. Education was of primary importance, I knew. So I applied myself diligently (I still do, and am continually "sharpening the saw," as Stephen Covey recommends). The Scotsman in my father had made it very clear that this was expected.

I have great appreciation for the influence that my father had on my life. Those lost years without a father's presence are part of a global tragedy of lost years for so many families, past and present. While they are deeply regrettable, they may provide some foundation for greater compassion and understanding among all people throughout the world.

Frank Nisbet, 1932

CHAPTER TEN

COMPASSION

Postscript: Java's Hidden Influence

I have often wondered, as the layers of my life unfold, at the influence of my formative years in Japanese concentration camps. How did they shape my outlook since the war living my life in Britain, the Caribbean, the United States, and Mexico? But I wonder, too, about the threads that drew my family into this region of war and captivity. What a seemingly winding road we took to end up there.

My mother, at the time that she met my father in Mexico, was in that country because she was searching for her own mother, whom she had seen only sporadically over the years since she was a five-year-old girl living in Honolulu. After her English-born mother, Nellie Kitchler (née Venus), had left her American-born father, Albert Kitchler, my mother was placed in a Hawaiian boarding school in Honolulu run by French nuns while her father traveled the Pacific islands on business. Her lonely childhood did not improve when my grandfather remarried an English society lady—who used my then twelve-year-old mother as a Cinderella-style serving girl at her fancy tea parties while excluding her from her father's life as much as possible. My mother attended various schools, including Punahou School, for many years, but finally graduated from the convent high school determined to find her own mother, who was then working as a journalist and English teacher in Mexico City. Nellie K., as she was called, wanted nothing to do with her daughter. It was friends of Nellie's who took my mother in, introduced her to a lawyer friend from Texas, a Mr. Bosch who had an office in Mexico City and who needed a secretary, a position my mother ably filled with her typing skills for the next six years, and eventually led her to the social gathering where she encountered the man who was soon to be her husband.

After political and economic events propelled my family from Mexico to the Far East to the Dutch East Indies, even more dramatic world events then resulted in our separation and internment. Although this experience was certainly not of our choosing, we were inexorably linked to a world web of circumstances that caught us in its grip. I am convinced that a universal order of some strange dimension chooses our parents, or maybe we choose them to learn certain lessons.

From our first breath, we breathe from a Universe and breathe back to a Universe that connects us all. Through my yoga and meditation practices as an adult, I have come to realize that interconnectedness of all matter and thought is a universal principle of life. I am intrigued by the concept of a cosmos so sensitive to our behaviors as to magnetize us toward our circumstances, choices, and experiences.

THE PAST IN THE PRESENT

It is fascinating to me how not only actions but also words and sentiments from one time and place resonate in others. A Hawaiian nanny of my mother's, for example, woke her each morning with the cheery missive to "see something beautiful, hear something beautiful, and say something beautiful today"—which years later helped buoy my mother, brother, and me in tougher times. And it was my mother's continual reminder to me that there were "good and bad in all races" that contributed to my marrying a West Indian man and, to this day, to be passionately interested in different peoples, cultures, and spiritual traditions, always considering my home to be "wherever I am in the world."

Of course, troublesome events and emotions resonate, just as do positive ones. The deep dread of authority figures that Captain Sonei's tirades and tenko days instilled in me was something I struggled with for many years. I have noted that I often feared dominating men, but even a strong-willed woman could scare me silly. Right after the war we lived with my father's strong and severe mother, Gran. She insisted I was never again to speak Dutch—which she equated with a terrible time in my life. Although I spoke Dutch fluently and English only haltingly, my fear of consequences caused me—literally—to forget an entire language instantly.

But sometimes, even traces of damage can evolve into newfound strengths. The discomfort that my fear of authority initially caused me in the workplace eventually helped me to find mentors in leadership who showed me how to be creative and thrive within a healthy organization. With the help of counselor and facilitator Cathie Sunshine, among others, the Fitness Department at the Ranch became what I consider a model of collaboration, creativity, and shared accomplishments. I learned that simply doing something affirmative, such as taking the time to review and post the positive guest comments for the whole staff to see each week, instilled a sense of pride and self-confidence in all. Sincere and well-deserved praise, as it turns out, is a far more effective motivator than fear.

As for men per se, I have been fortunate to meet many good ones over the years—those who enjoy the company of men and women equally. In my second marriage, I wed a delightful musician, Herbert Hecht, who totally allowed me to be who I am and with whom I evolved a partnership of kindliness and love in which we both flourished and blossomed. I feel very fortunate to have experienced this for fifteen years: a truly egalitarian relationship that delighted us both. Herb died in 2000, leaving a very happy legacy and memory, although I miss him dearly.

I should also note that my best spiritual teachers have been men: Reverend Berry, the Methodist minister in Essex who taught us comparative religion in Sunday school; Shinzen Young, my Vipassana teacher in Los Angeles; and the Dalai Lama, whose teachings I attended in Dharamsala, India, and Pasadena, California. My best professional exemplars have been mostly women and include the principles of schools I attended or worked in as a teacher: Miss Leworthy, Mrs. Mitchell in London, Mrs. Lynch in Barbados, and of course Deborah Szekely, cofounder of Rancho la Puerta where I currently work. They have all been my mentors and a source of inspiration over the years directly and even indirectly by example.

In spiritual matters, as in personal relationships and professional matters, I have learned the importance of heeding my own best instincts. If old fears and self-doubts rear their heads, I recall what the Sufi poet and mystic Kabir says: "Let go of all imaginary things and stand firm in that which you are." As for the once life-saving advice of my mother's to "bow and what you think is your own business," the Biblical saying, "Be as wise as serpents, yet gentle as doves," is probably closer to what I do now, rather than just keeping quiet and saying nothing when I see an injustice or have a constructive idea.

CHILD'S POSE

I have mentioned that my yoga practice has helped me to find a coherent, even comforting perspective on life's seemingly random events. It continues to do this and more as the years go by.

Yoga has been an integral part of my life since I was twenty-two. However, I was first introduced to it by my mother, who practiced it from a book by Indra Devi, Yoga for Americans. I was sixteen when she began to practice, but was much too busy with school studies and sports to take an interest. Yoga hardly had the kind of following in Essex, England, in the 1950s as it has worldwide today, but it was fascinating for me to learn at a later date that during that era that guests from Rancho la Puerta walked to Indra Devi's ashram two miles away from the Ranch to practice yoga and meditation with her.

It wasn't until I married Torrey in 1957 that my own fascination with yoga took hold. I was absorbed with my geography studies at London University and also with the study of comparative religions and the impact of sacred and historical geography on the lives of people around the world. My geography field studies, along with spiritual studies, inevitably intersected with the study of yoga. ("Geography is the meeting ground of many disciplines," one geography lecturer was fond of quoting. And so is yoga the yoking together of many disciplines.)

Torrey helped open the yogic door for me by bringing people from diverse parts of the globe to our home in London and giving me the opportunity to learn what made them tick. Our guests shared with us their belief systems and spiritual practices. It was one of these friends, having just returned from India where she'd lived in an ashram for six months, who introduced us to the practice of yoga in 1958—beginning with a headstand. I loved it instantly. Hand in hand with yoga came meditation and a deepening of my interest in the world's wisdom traditions. The dual exploration of my outer space through geography and inner space through yoga and meditation blended together and continue to do so to this day, fifty years later.

What drew me to yoga with such zeal? My own worldview, shaped—through "accident" of birth and circumstance—by exposure to so many cultures at an early age, was such that yoga attracted me like a magnet. Yoga is about uniting all the seemingly disparate aspects of oneself, and I had many aspects to unite.

The physical practice of yoga, with its concept of "movement as metaphor" expressed in the different asana, or postures, has helped me process my life story with greater clarity. The standing poses are rooted to the earth, offering a firm foundation, not only for my body, but also for my life, giving deeper meaning to Kabir's statement, "Stand firm in that which you are." This resonates in my mind and heart every time I practice the warrior poses, hold my ground, and face the vicissitudes of life with courage and boldness. Forward bends tuned me into my own inner wisdom with patience and stillness, and backbends served not only to strengthen my back but also to open my heart. The ultimate pose of supplication and surrender to the inner wisdom is child's pose, a pose of rest and looking inward, and also a pose of humility.

Phyllis in Warrior II pose

You are not a different person when practicing yoga than you are in real life. The discipline of practicing yoga daily has served me well in facing my personal challenges: divorce, moving to a different country, the death of my second husband, to name just a few over the past several decades. When I most need grounding in the face of loss or difficulty, I draw sustenance from the mountain pose. The mountain pose is the quintessential pose of both stillness and strength: standing like a mountain, both feet planted firmly on the earth while the top of your head reaches to the heavens. Returning to mountain pose after a demanding sequence of poses offers the opportunity to witness oneself returning to stillness and observing how quickly one can accomplish that. This return to stillness, or spiritual recovery rate, in the yoga poses can be a practice in life after a sudden trauma or shock.

The evolution of my yoga practice from purely physical poses at the age of twenty-two to an inner expression of spirit through movement at the age of seventy-two has given me a deeper sense of purpose and identity in the world. With this deepening appreciation of the power of the present moment flowing smoothly together through breath and movement, comes a better experience of the flow of life and my part in it.

THE DISTANT MIRROR OF MEMORY

My decision to write this story came to me while my mother visited me at Rancho la Puerta in 1995. We were discussing memories of our concentration camp experience with a friend of mine. I recalled picking leaves and flowers that could be added to our cooking pot to add more nutrients to our collective meals in the packed house we shared with sixty other women and children. "It wasn't like that at all," my mother burst out in shocked anger. "That would have been far too dangerous."

How could our memories be so different? I calmed her down. "I must be confusing the memories of those three years," I told her. "After all, I was between five and nine years old. I have vivid memories of picking flowers with someone, and you've often told the story of the Burmese woman in the last camp collecting edible flowers and plants to add to our cooking pot. Perhaps I put those two together over the years. So, if it wasn't the Burmese woman, who did I walk with to pick flowers, and when?" "You children did a lot of things on your own" she replied, "I was working hard at the tasks the Japanese had allocated us." "Well, perhaps I did go with her and we just did not tell you," I suggested. "I remember being told about hibiscus flowers especially."

"The Burmese lady and I would collect edible plants early in the morning and you never came with us," my mother countered. "Before we were actually interned, our good friend Auntie Vena took you for nature walks. Perhaps your memory is linked to that experience. She loved flowers and tried to teach you their names as you strolled past the neighborhood gardens. In fact, you were only five at the time and had the utmost difficulty saying hibiscus. You called them 'his biscuits' for years."

"I remember the beautiful gardens and the hibiscus flowers," I replied. "And I have many other memory snippets of those war years. Perhaps I have mixed up many more memories in relation to their time lines. Who knows? My friends are always so interested in hearing my story of the concentration camp years, our circumstances and family history. Of course, I can only tell them what I think I remember! Maybe we should get together sometime and get it all straight. At least we can unravel our experiences together and I can get a fuller explanation of what happened."

I was quite eager to know more about my mother's memories. As an adult during those years, she would doubtless have clearer recollections than I.

A year later, I visited my mother in Spain for a week's vacation. She gamely went over the war years, flushing out each of my vignettes with a fuller tale. I recorded over three hours of stories and memories.

I learned a great deal about those years from our exchange. Her vivid explanations and descriptions also explained a number of unresolved questions in my mind. One in particular bothered me a great deal in my adult years. "Why did I have so few horrifying memories of the concentration camps, especially in Tjideng, with its notorious reputation?" All through my young teenage years growing up in Britain my answer to questions such as, "What was it like to be in a concentration camp?" was always, "It wasn't so bad. The Japanese usually left the women and children alone." I might even venture, "And not all the guards were bad. I remember one good one who gave us his fruit ration as prizes for running races." How could I have the impression that those years were not so bad? I read articles and books by women who recalled the atrocities of those years living in the same camps that I had been in. Their stories filled me with horror. Where was I during those times? Did my young mind blank them out so completely, refusing to acknowledge or remember them?

"I tried to keep you and your brother Donald away from the worst acts by the Japanese," my mother explained. "You were not present at many of the worst situations. We were fortunate in the last camp, Tjideng, to be located in a house at the very outskirts of the camp. I instructed you both to stay there and play all day in the care of the older Burmese woman in our house. The main hullabaloo took place in the central area of the camp by the main gate. Our house was far from there, so you rarely saw what went on."

What a challenge my mother rose to—keeping my brother and me safe, and shielding us as best she could from the stark realities of our situation. Her ingenuity, tenacity, and common sense still remain in her mid nineties. When she recently insisted on moving from one retirement home in Dumfries, Scotland, to another, she adamantly insisted, "I don't mind dying of old age, but I sure as hell am not willing to die of boredom."

I look back with deep appreciation at what my mother has given me over the years; a survival instinct of my own with an ability to weather many different and often difficult circumstances in my own life, some of my own creation and others not; an insatiable curiosity about the world, different cultures and nationalities; and an ability to tell stories with humor and flair. All of these my mother gave me through osmosis. Experiencing these qualities in her and now knowing them to be inside of me as well is the consummate mother-daughter bond. And I am grateful that the spirit of many bold, proactive, adventurous women runs in my blood.

My personal story has, I hope, many more chapters. Like my mother, I try to hold onto optimism about the future—not just mine, but everyone's. Yet I am saddened by the continual ugliness of war today. As I conclude this book, it is the year 2009, and the people of the world are no nearer to world peace than we were sixty-four years ago. Innocent children and families continue to be the victims of national aggressions in Europe, Africa, South America, and Asia. Ethnic cleansing seems to be the order of the day. It appalls me. What ails the human spirit that a handful of men in power insist on controlling others against their will, bludgeoning them into submission or performing genocide? I have no answers to these questions. Only a deep cry from inside of me to shout to the world, "Stop this madness. Love one another. Help one another. Create beauty and harmony, not ugliness and hatred. Is that so difficult?"

My own experience tells me that it is better to be free than to be imprisoned, that it is better to have choices and take responsibility for them than to have none and be subjugated by the choices of others; that the collective good of people working together in collaboration and harmony is preferable to dictatorship; and that love and compassion are preferable to hatred, cruelty, and vindictiveness. I hope for a better world, and in my small way work toward creating it.

CHAPTER ELEVEN

DESTINY

FEPOW ASSOCIATION AND ABCIFER

In 1994 in Britain, a small group of survivors of the Japanese concentration camps met to form an organization called the Far East Prisoner of War Association, or FEPOW. They were to represent a total numbering eighteen thousand British survivors. My mother signed up members of our family and notified me of my membership. I paid annual dues until it was officially closed in 2007. Their main task on behalf of their members along with another organization called the Association of British Civilian Internees—Far East Region (ABCIFER) repeatedly appealed to the Japanese government for both an apology and compensation for the cruel treatment meted out to them during the internment years from 1941–45. The appeals were either ignored or refused on the basis that they had absolution from any further responsibility for POWs after their final capitulation and signing of a peace treaty in San Francisco in 1951. Although the Japanese did apologize for the misery caused, they offered no monetary compensation. Appeals continued with visits to Japan and Japanese embassies to meet directly with Japanese authorities to personally make their claim. Although the FEPOW and ABCIFER representatives were received politely, again only a verbal apology was ever offered by embassy officials.

In 1998, ABCIFER unearthed the terms of the San Francisco Peace Treaty of 1951. The forty-seven-year-old treaty, conveniently forgotten for all those years, was now open for all to read. It transpired that the Japanese government, as a signer of the peace treaty, did pay £4,500,000 compensation to the Red Cross to be paid to the Allied governments for citizens of the latter who had been held in captivity during World War II in the Far East. All the governments, presumably strapped for money in the postwar years, chose to keep the money instead of passing it onto their citizens. With this revelation, the Canadian, Australian, and New Zealand governments immediately passed laws to recompense their citizens.

The British government lagged egregiously and did not respond immediately. The outrage of this reluctance to admit their responsibility to survivors galvanized the FEPOW and ABCIFER representatives to appeal directly to the British government for immediate compensation for what was their due.

By November 2000, British Prime Minister Tony Blair finally authorized the payment of £10,000 to each British citizen who had been in a Japanese concentration camp during the Second World War. The monetary amount was based on the precedent set by the United States government in 1988, to compensate $20,000 to those U.S. citizens of Japanese descent who, while living in the United States, had been interned in concentration camps in California and Hawaii during the Second World War.

The British minister of defense was to work out the details. That was the right thing to do, said Blair. I submitted my application for compensation, listing the names of the concentration camps I had lived in, and naming my father (a British citizen), mother, and brother as my relatives who had been in the same situation. I received a check for £10,000 in the year 2001.

The minister of defense, however, created a definition of "British" that excluded thousands of British citizens from this compensation. The definition stated that to be British, each person would have to be born in Great Britain, in the sense of the actual European country, or have a parent or grandparent who had been born there. But many of the British who had been interned in the Far East were descended from diplomats, plantation owners, or businessmen who had left Great Britain–proper several generations earlier to live and work in Malaya, Borneo, and Hong Kong—the internees were British by blood and owned British passports as members of the British Empire. "British enough to be interned by the Japanese, but not British enough to get compensation," was the outcry from ABCIFER.

The minister of defense was adamant and would not budge on this definition of "British" until June 2006, when a twenty-year amendment was added to the bloodline rule, redefining qualifications for compensation based on postwar residency. The amendment stated that any British POW held by the Japanese in the Far East during World War II who had subsequently lived in the United Kingdom for at least twenty years between 1945 and November 2000 would qualify for compensation. It was implemented immediately. However, this still left thousands out of the loop, who were technically British but did not live in the UK.

Further appeals from ABCIFER have continued for the past three years to no avail. Suspicion was voiced that the ministry of defense hoped that the problem would go away as the applicants died from old age. This disgraceful problem still exists to this day, with lawyers continuing to appeal to the Ministry of Defense. The slogan for those few remaining citizens continues: "British enough to be interned, but not British enough to get compensation." The appeal continues to fall on deaf ears.

PACIFIC OCEAN

BANDAR SERI BEGAWAN

BRUNEI

SUMATRA

KALIMANTAN
BORNEO

⊙ Balakpapan

MALUKU

SULAWESI

IRIAN JAYA

⊙ Jakarta

JAVA

NUSA TENGGARA

BALI

FLORES

LOMBOK

KOMODO
& RINCA

EAST TIMOR

PAPUA NEW GUINEA

INDIAN OCEAN

1938 Nisbet family moved from
Tampico/Mexico to Balakpapan/Borneo

1939 Nisbet family moved from
Balakpapan/Borneo to Tjepoe/Java

JAVA SEA

JAKARTA
Tjideng Camp

BANDOENG
First 3 Camps

TJEPOE

Sarangan (Hill Station)

CILACAP
Bombing of Port

SOLO

1942 The Journey across Java:
- Tjepoe to Sarangan by car and donkey
- Sarangan to Solo by donkey and on foot
- Solo to Cilacap by train
- Cilacap to Bandoeng by car

1943 • Bandoeng to Jakarta by cattle train

RANCHO LA PUERTA

Tecate • Baja California • Mexico

Rancho La Puerta
Fitness Resort and Spa
Tecate, Baja California, Mexico

The Ranch has offered a place and space for many thousands of guests over the 69 years since its founding in 1940. Nestled at the foot of sacred Mount Kuchumaa it continues to offer a safe haven for both vigorous exercise and quieter inner reflection and meditation and gentler movement disciplines.

Phyllis arrived in 1981 to teach yoga and has stayed to work at the Ranch over the past 28 years. In addition to her duties as a yoga instructor and managing the fitness department for over 18 years, she used some of her leisure hours to reflect on her life and sift out the many twists and turns that have brought her to this moment in this remarkable place – perfect for inner reflection.

Yoga and hiking mountains has always been her passion. The Ranch offers expansive views and inner / outer discovery. The beautiful gardens and exquisite cuisine add to the delight and wonder of this place she has called home for almost a third of her life. It is where she was able to write about her early life in Japanese Concentration Camps in Java with help from many of the Ranch's guests over the years.

"The Ranch is a wonderful place to visit. Why not consider a week's healthful vacation? We can meet, and perhaps enjoy a chat about life after a swim or on a vegetable garden walk, or a stroll through the award winning gardens.

"It would be my pleasure to share the Ranch with you. Maybe you will find your muse here and write about your life. The Ranch has done that for many writers and poets in the past. An enchanting world awaits you."

www.rancholapuerta.com

Phyllis Pilgrim, Dorothy and Donald Nisbet, June 2009

ABOUT THE AUTHOR

PHYLLIS PILGRIM
was born in Tampico, Mexico of an
American mother and a Scottish father
who worked for the Shell Oil Company.
Later transferred to Borneo and Java
where her brother Donald was born,
they were captured by the Japanese
after Pearl Harbor where Phyllis from
the age of 5 to 9 years along with her
mother and brother were interned

in civilian internment camps for 3½ years until 1945. The
family survived, returned to England where Phyllis started her
education and eventually gained a degree in Geography from
University College, London. She married a Barbadian and has
a son, Owen from that marriage. She taught Geography in high
schools in London and Barbados for 24 years. In 1981, Phyllis left
Barbados to work as a yoga teacher at Rancho La Puerta, in Tecate,
Mexico where she still teaches and directs the "Specialty and
Spirit Week" programs. She currently lives in San Diego, enjoys
visiting her son Owen and his family, and especially her young
granddaughter, Sydney. She also travels the world for her vacations,
trekking in Tibet, Bhutan, Tasmania, Peru, Africa, and the Lake
District in England among many other places.